Contents

Evaluating and Assessing Drama

Drama_works_ focuses on planning drama, creating practical structures and developing drama pretexts. Methods of reflecting on and evaluating the work are built into the pretexts. In our next book *Mapping Drama* we again present a series of practical drama structures but shift the focus from planning onto realistic ways of evaluating, assessing, recording and reporting progress in drama.

D1328744

3

Introduction

This book really began its life imperceptibly as the two of us taught, thought, planned, ran and discussed drama in our various jobs, roles and capacities as drama practitioners over a period of ten years. We found that some of the drama structures we created with our groups and classes were 'classics'. We enjoyed repeating them as the years passed. Most importantly, each time we used them they improved. It was as though the structures we had created with our groups had become, to us, drama education texts in their own right.

When we passed them on to each other and to colleagues, some of whom suddenly found themselves teaching drama, we found that they worked for them as well. They said the structures were realistic in not attempting to achieve the impossible in every session; that although no such text can ever guarantee success these gave them time to develop their own skills as drama practitioners. One teacher quoted the old maxim, 'It is not only what you do but also how you do it'. She said the structures freed her up from the immediacy of 'what' and provided an opportunity to focus on the 'how' and 'why' of drama. We also used the structures with other age groups including undergraduates, postgraduates and specific groups in the community including prisoners.

The structures became for us more than just lesson plans. They had the feel of artistic as well as educational creations. They had their own aesthetic. Cecily O'Neill speaking at an international conference for practitioners of drama education, used the word 'pre-text' to describe this sort of work [1]. We interpret this to be a well constructed scaffolding structure for drama. A text that allows groups to quickly engage in drama and then create their own quality drama within and from that liberating structure. A pretext.[2]

Drama education practitioners and writers have been involved in this for years. They have produced structures that have stood the test of time. Such structures have often been presented to illustrate points about the drama process, but they are still used because of the unique way in which form, process and content have been fused [3].

At the core of this book sit five pretexts with a sixth in the section called 'Developing a drama pretext' (page 99). We have used them, and continue to use them, to generate drama and theatre that engages, challenges and excites groups of all abilities and ages. Resource lists are included.

Preceding them is a section (page 5) which looks at the fundamental question of *why* we think drama education is so important in the classroom and what the group potentially gets from the experience. It then describes the practical ways in which drama can be structured.

Following the pretexts is a section (page 99) which explores how you can plan and create your own pretexts. An extensive illustrative book list is included for those interested in finding out more about drama education.

We believe that volumes of drama pretexts should sit next to volumes of play texts. Instead of rooting through text books for examples and then apologising for using someone else's plans, the teacher can credit the pretext written for the classroom/studio/community space, with an author. She can then set about using, exploring and creating from it in just the way practitioners have been doing for years with copies of play texts written for the stage.

The pretexts in this book *work*. They offer time to the busy teacher, lecturer, practitioner. What we also hope is that practitioners, pupils and students develop the ability to create their own pretexts and to make meaning of and celebrate life through their drama.

Drama*works*

*Planning drama • Creating practical structures
• Developing drama pretexts*

Drama*works* focuses on planning drama, creating practical structures and developing drama pretexts. At the core of the book sit six pretexts that have been used and continue to be used to generate drama and theatre which engages, challenges and excites groups of all ages and abilities.

ALLAN OWENS & KEITH BARBER

Allan Owens is Senior Lecturer in Drama and Theatre Studies at University College, Chester. Prior to this, he worked in secondary and community schools, further education and the advisory service. He currently teaches on B.A., M.A., B.Ed, M.Ed, P.G.C.E. (Secondary and Primary Drama) courses and is an OFSTED Inspector for drama. Through this work he continues to practise drama in all phases of education and in the community.

Keith Barber is Head of Lower School and Head of Drama at Victoria Community High School, Crewe, Cheshire. He has extensive experience of teaching at secondary and primary level. He is currently responsible for primary liaison and this involves him in regularly teaching drama in all of the partnership primary schools.

02

Dedication

To our mums, dads, Clare, Caz and the kids.

Acknowledgements

We owe much to a whole host of writers on drama which we hope is adequately acknowledged in the text and illustrative book list.

This book represents our personal view of drama but this has inevitably been shaped by particular individuals and groups. Whilst they cannot and may not want to be held responsible for the work, we would like to gratefully acknowledge their encouragement and influence.

All of the pupils, students, members of the community and colleagues who have worked with us over the years; Drama and Education staff at University College Chester, and Victoria Community High School, Crewe; Simon Taylor and all the Cheshire Drama Education Services team; Jonothan Neelands, Warwick University; Rose Dickenson, H.M. Prison Styal; Erkki Laakso and students at the University of Jyväskylä, Finland; lastly thanks to Alan Turner for his patience and help in formatting the first draft.

> In the text of this book, when referring to the teacher we have used 'he' and 'she' in equal amounts. This has been done to avoid a gender imbalance which would go against the spirit of the work.

Published by Carel Press Ltd, 4 Hewson Street, Carlisle, Tel 01228 38928
©1997 Allan Owens & Keith Barber
Cover and inside design: Paul Cunningham
Printed by MFP Ltd, Manchester
Printing number: 1 2 3 4 5 6 7 8 9 10
ENVIRONMENTAL INFORMATION
The book is printed on 100% recycled paper which is made entirely from printed waste, & is not re-bleached. Using recycled paper saves trees, water & energy, & reduces air pollution & landfill.

British Library Cataloguing in Publication Data
Owens, Allan
DRAMAworks: successful drama pretexts across the age range
1. Drama – Study and teaching
I. Title   II. Barber, Keith
792.07
ISBN 1-872365-32-9

Why should I use drama education?

Before looking at **how** we plan for drama, we need to ask an even more fundamental question:- '**Why** should I use drama in my classroom/studio/space?' The reasons given will vary from individual to individual. In each case this will have a direct bearing on 'what' is planned for and 'how' this is planned. We will try to answer this from four angles relating to values, pragmatism, empirical evidence and political reasoning. Having clarified our position, we hope to demonstrate how ideas can be developed into drama pretexts.

Four key reasons

First of all, **values** (what we believe in). No matter how hard you try, it is difficult to stop children playing. We believe that the human need to symbolise meaning through art forms and through imaginative play should be utilised. By giving children and adults the opportunity to 'take their play seriously', we create the opportunity for a **powerful form of learning in context**. We enjoy it, they enjoy it!

Secondly, **pragmatic reasons** (it works in our circumstances). Time and time again we have seen drama work with groups whose ages and abilities might initially make us sceptical as to its use — with four year olds just about to enter school, with disaffected 16 year olds, with prisoners. It has worked in our circumstances as **a motivating force for learning.**

Thirdly, **empirical data** (we have evidence that this delivers). The pretexts presented have been used many times in many sorts of classrooms, studios, and community settings. Their existence and the continued demand for their use provides evidence on a simple level that drama 'delivers'. From the beginning of the century, the government department responsible for education has acknowledged the role drama can play in the learning process. So, for example, HMI in *The Teaching and Learning of Drama* provide many examples of good practice to support their claim that drama can promote quality learning:

'Where it is done well, the teaching of drama has a strong influence upon the development of language and literacy, and the children's self-confidence. Drama also

often helps them towards a greater awareness and understanding of inter-personal skills and social relationships'. [4]

All of these reports, to varying degrees, have implied that **drama can promote 'quality learning'**. What is this? It is not a diet of transmission and reproduction with the simple acquiring and storage of knowledge as the driving rationale. The implication is that children, just like adults, learn in various ways. They have preferred learning styles, but to depend on just one style such as transmission and reproduction (you sit still and learn the things I tell you) actually stops individuals wanting to learn. It is just as ridiculous to suggest that active learning mediums such as drama are the only way we can 'really' learn (learning by doing).

There is a lot of 'sit-stillery' in our education system [5]. Drama pretexts aim to provide, like any good teacher, a range of learning styles, activities and physical groupings. They make demands on the emotional, physical and intellectual capacities of individuals in the group.

The fourth reason why we use drama is **political**: because **the drama process can be empowering**.

Drama education practice from the beginning of this century has sought to promote a culture of learner-centred learning in the form of a social and collective art form. Good teachers of drama have never been simply 'facilitators'. They also have a knowledge of, and enthusiasm for, their subject area. Methods promoted for adult learners are those which have been at the heart of drama education practice from its earliest roots.

'We...(Ruskin College Oxford), promote a culture of learning as a collective enterprise in which tutors have certain knowledges that they offer while opening these to critical review and consideration and which draw considerably on students' experience and prior and developing understanding. Quality teaching which communicates complicated ideas and generates action and critical thinking and discussion is greatly valued. Yet teaching is not directly equatable with 'having the knowledge'. In fact good teaching opens up questions of what is knowledge, who generates it and who benefits?' [6]

Teaching drama in this sense is potentially **a democratic and critical activity**. Pretexts seek to promote individual thinking in the face of group and received opinion. As Jonothan Neelands has often quoted, *'If you don't stand for something you'll fall for anything.'* [7]

The social and cultural roots of drama education

As far as we can tell, drama has been part of our society and culture from the beginnings of civilisation. From the moment man and woman started to try to understand and celebrate the world they lived in, they danced, drew and acted out their perceptions, thoughts and feelings. Children who are by definition 'new to the world' have always done this quite naturally.

By the time a child is one year old, he or she will follow another's line of regard to see what they are looking at. This interest in what others look at and think becomes the basis for imitative play in the early years of our lives. Educational psychologists such as Jerome Bruner and Margaret Donaldson suggest that the very youngest children do have the capacity to take another's perspective as long as they understand the situation in which that person is operating. Drama can provide this context. [8]

In institutional terms, drama education in Britain can be traced back to the work of Henry Caldwell Cook in 1917 and Harriet Finlay Johnson in 1923. As a movement in education it really has been developed by a stream of practitioners from 1945 onwards. These include Peter Slade, Brian Way, Dorothy Heathcote, Gavin Bolton and Jonothan Neelands. Many countries around the world have looked at the way we use drama education and we in turn draw upon the work of practitioners such as David Booth (Canada) and John O'Toole (Australia). [9]

The Drama Education Process
– A basic vocabulary

Our definition of drama and theatre is intended to be inclusive. It places them on the same continuum with the proviso that the quality of the experience of all the participants is central to the drama education process. It is now increasingly recognised that work of quality can be generated through a whole range of approaches in drama and theatre and therapy. [10]

Having a shared vocabulary that enables drama education practioners, their students and pupils to talk about their subject is important if there is to be any meaningful dialogue about work. A general problem with any specialist vocabulary is that a point can be reached where the terminology employed becomes so esoteric that it actively blocks understanding. Rather than aiding, it becomes jargon which alienates instead of assisting.

There is also a second difficulty in drama education, as no consistent shared vocabulary has ever been formally agreed at any point in its development this century. Analysis reveals a rich diversity, or confusing uncertainty, depending on your point of view.

What follows is a basic vocabulary for this book, identifying those words and terms that are the roots of our drama practice. It is not definitive or exclusive.

Drama and Theatre –

the definition we use is *'We do, we struggle to make meaning and share this through pretence'*. As in any worthwhile struggle, there are moments of difficulty, risk, challenge and celebration. A particular factor of this struggle is that the 'doing' is social and collective and based on play. (The root of the word drama is the Greek word *drao* meaning 'a thing done'.) By 'pretence' is meant the *as-if* mode. They act *as-if* they were someone else or somewhere else, that something is about to happen or has just happened.

Sometimes the group members agree to pretend to create meaning just for themselves as a group. At other times they agree to share this with others who have not been part of the process, through performance. The emphasis is then on the audience (which may be either in the group or not) seeing, hearing, 'reading' the event. (The root of the word theatre is the Greek word *theatron* derived from the verb *theasthai* meaning 'to see'. Originally 'theatre' referred not to a locality but simply to the assembled group of onlookers). [11]

The Drama Contract

is formed when a teacher and a group enter into an agreement to do something on mutually agreed and binding terms. A **short term** contract could be for one session in which the main role of the contract is to give the group ownership of the drama. This could involve them in making decisions about form and content. A **long term** contract could be the length of the whole time the teacher and group are to work together, for example one year, in which details are agreed as to how the teacher and the group should work together and how the working relationship could develop.

At its simplest level, the teacher asks if the group feels they could work in a particular way on a specific subject. To an inexperienced group she might say, *'I promise I will not make you do anything you really do not feel comfortable with, on the other hand the drama can't happen unless you contribute. Do you think we could have a go at this and see what happens?'* If there really is antagonism or total lack of willingness to co-operate, the contract cannot operate and the drama cannot realistically begin. If, at any point in the drama, either the teacher or group feel the drama is not working, they have the right to stop the work and discuss ways forward. The contract can be written and tied in with a negotiated way of working or simply be verbally acknowledged.

Belief

occurs when there is a trust and confidence in the unfolding events of the drama. The participants can see the distinction between fiction and reality. This gives them an assurance which allows the drama to be taken seriously.

Commitment

is a willingness to try to build belief in a drama. This implies that a person is willing to submit decisions to the collective whole of the group without losing individual responses. Because drama is a social and collective art form, individuals agree to restrict certain freedoms of action in order that something bigger than the sum parts of the whole can be created.

Social Health

is concerned with how members of the group work together as a whole and how individuals operate within it. Good social health implies, for example, that the group can co-operate together very well and have a high individual tolerance level. Members of a group with poor social health find it difficult, even impossible, to work together for even the shortest period of time. They are intolerant towards each other. This can make a drama very difficult and restrict any meaningful development.

Protection into Drama

happens when participants find themselves comfortably engaged in a drama which they would usually find embarrassing or difficult. The teacher does this by carefully negotiating, renegotiating and selecting appropriate form and content with the group. The pretexts in this book reflect this.

Role

asks, of the participant, *'Who am I?'* or *'Who are we?'* in the drama. For example in the pretext *Rogan's Fair* (page 45) – *'We are travelling fairground workers'*. (At times, emphasis in drama will be on the ability to adopt multiple roles and perspectives. In this case individuals are 'freed from the responsibilities of characterisation'. [12] At other times when developments from the pretext have led to performance, the emphasis will shift to that of sustained characterisation and associated demands).

Situation

asks *'Where am I?'* or *'Where are we?'* in the drama. For example in *Rogan's Fair* – *'We are in a field, it is early evening'*.

Focus

asks *'What am I (or 'What are we) concerned about at this moment of action?'*. For example in *Rogan's Fair* – *'We are concerned that our rides and stalls are securely loaded on the lorries. We are doing a last check.'*

Perspective

can relate to role, situation and focus. 'What is it important for us to know prior to this moment of action?' For example, in *Rogan's Fair* – *'This is the end of the travelling season. We are tired but looking forward to moving to our last site of the year where we usually make enough money to see us through the winter months.'*

Drama Conventions

are an agreed way of structuring a dramatic encounter, through the use of space, action and time, to create meaning. [13] The names given to conventions are no more than shorthand titles for communication. Instead of saying, *'Half of us line up facing the other half, and then we'll let the character walk down between us and try to influence the decision she must have made before she reaches the end'*, we simply say, *'Tunnel of decision/conscience corridor/conscience alley'*. In good practice, conventions are used dynamically and are an integral part of the fabric of the whole session. If used mechanistically, the drama becomes no more than a 'painting by numbers' exercise.

Drama Elements

these are component parts of any drama. They are the basics of the art, e.g.

Tension:

maintenance of a high degree of active engagement and excitement. The group may know what is going to happen but the structure of the drama makes the actual unfolding of action inherently and increasingly interesting.

Contrast:

sudden or gradual changes of role, situation, focus and/or perspective used to change the mood and pace of the drama.

Symbol:

when an object, word, gesture or setting is endowed with a special significance for one or all of the participants or spectators.

Metaphor:

enables the participants and spectators to see different levels of meaning within the drama and to see the connections with their own lives and the perceived lives of others.

Metaxis:

is the process of running two worlds together simultaneously: that of everyday life and that of the unfolding drama. The feelings and thoughts that are thus generated encourage a particular quality of insight. [14]

Drama Form

is the overall arrangement of the dramatic engagement. This involves selecting appropriate genre, (and conventions, frame and elements to suit the chosen approach). e.g. Theatre in Education, partner in role, forum, mantle of the expert.

Drama Skills

involve a practised ability in the techniques of drama and theatre e.g. the ability to manipulate form, develop a role, use gesture and language appropriate to the context of the drama etc.

Drama Frame

brings together all of the above facets, to clarify the moment of entry into a drama or another specific point in it.

Approaches to planning for drama

Drama is a disciplined business and planning is part of it. You would not expect to just launch into any other subject or topic area without thinking through your approach and the same is true for drama. Some practitioners say: *'Oh I just ask them what they want to do and then go with that.'* This may work if you are tremendously experienced and know the group well. If you are just starting to teach drama, the security of a plan will probably make you feel more relaxed. If you are relaxed you will be able to listen to what the students are saying through the drama; there will be more chance of you creating a drama together than there will be if you are worrying about the practical aspects of starting work. Rather than stifling the group's creativity you are providing a structure, a pretext, to release and give it shape.

In the following section we identify four overall approaches to planning for drama. The one(s) chosen depends to a large degree on the experience of the teacher and of the group.

1 The choice of the content can be given over to the group

Subject matter would be their choice. The teacher would ask them literally *'What would you like to do a drama about next week?'*

Advantages

The group members have a real sense of ownership of the content, it means something to them and so they are likely to be motivated. It keeps the teacher working on new ideas and is in this sense a creative and educational challenge. The teacher would largely be responsible for form but, in establishing the contract, would share the choice of conventions and elements with the group in order to build their knowledge of handling these in future work, e.g. they might ask to do some drama on a subject such as the environment.

Disadvantages

The group may disagree with each other about content and lose interest in the work because their idea has been rejected. Of course, handling of the drama contract is important here. The same 'clichéd content' (to the teacher, not necessarily the group) may appear again and again, e.g. the group may ask to do 'war' or 'robbing banks' or will simply name a soap or a video or film they have just watched and ask if they can 'do it'.

The group will soon get bored if they are left to imitate a soap or film in small groups. The teacher has the job of finding some way into that content that will give the students a feeling of success and also open up some learning areas in terms of skills, knowledge, and understanding. Advisory drama teachers often find they have to work in this way. For example, a phone call comes through and someone asks if the advisory teacher can come in and do some drama about 'wood' next Monday.

If a group is given the expectation that the teacher has to make the drama exciting for them, they can become lazy and the teacher exhausted, all doomed ultimately to failure as it is unlikely that anyone can provide a continuous stream of creative methods month after month on their own. An additional point is that what the class choose to do may not tie in with the curriculum.

2 The teacher can provide the initial content and the students develop this (with support about choices of form)

Advantages

This is an easier job in some ways for the teacher. The group have to negotiate their use of form and ultimately take the responsibility for making the drama work. Because the teacher has researched a topic, area, text or specific skill, the onus is on the group to reciprocate that effort. Well considered resources and information can hook the interest of the group quickly. The teacher is also committed to the stimulus and genuinely interested in what the group think of and do with the materials he has provided.

Disadvantages

At its worst this is a relinquishing of the teacher's responsibility for development of the group's drama and theatre skills, knowledge and understanding. Some examination boards still seem to encourage the idea of 'spontaneous improvisation' or 'spon-imp' as it has infamously become known. In this method of working the teacher does little or no research on content and simply says to the students something like: 'holiday' or 'conflict'. Small groups then launch into superficial, knock-about, rambling improvisations that are hastily shown at the end of a lesson.

More often than not there is not time to 'see' them all so a promise is made to look at those not seen in the next lesson. Usually someone from each of these remaining groups is absent due to illness and so they can't show their work or are given five minutes to work on it whilst everyone else gets bored. And then the whole business starts again with little comment from the teacher other than, *'They were very good, well done. Try not to turn your back to the audience, speak a little louder and don't go in the corner of the room away from your audience next time. Some good ideas'*.

It is not unknown for a teacher using this method to also say: *'I don't know what they're going to do with this piece. I know it's about drugs but they've been working on it themselves'*.

There is a fine line between encouraging autonomy and abdicating responsibility. Sometimes to physically survive as a teacher of drama we have to leave the group to their own devices whilst maintaining a supervisory role. If this, however, was the only diet the group had, their drama would remain, in all probability, superficial. How are they to learn about form in order to improve their practice? In other words, how are they going to improve at drama?

3 Teacher negotiates content and form with the students

Advantages

The group are well motivated as they have ownership of form and content. As this has been negotiated, the teacher may well have built in particular challenges and have been invited to intervene when he thinks appropriate. This is an option really open only to groups who are well grounded in the skills, knowledge, elements and forms of drama and theatre. This method of planning and working also gives the teacher a chance to stand back a little more from the group, to monitor and assess development. She can also challenge work when it becomes superficial or stereotypical.

The aim of this way of working is to give the group autonomy and responsibility whilst having the opportunity to draw on the teacher's experience when necessary. Teacher tends to operate as 'primus inter pares' – first amongst equals, a phrase which perhaps captures the essence of this method of planning and working.

If the group and/or the teacher do not have the experience and confidence to work in this method it can be a very frustrating way of working. Selection is an important skill in drama and securing mutual agreement on the way work should develop can be difficult and time consuming.

4 The teacher chooses initial content and form

Advantages

She creates a structure to generate a drama which the group then develops – a pretext. This is a carefully thought-out structure, usually based on work which has its origins in methods 1, 2 or 3 of planning. The teacher has seen the potential of this structure and identified it as a viable scheme of work, usually for a half term. In the pretext, key learning outcomes in terms of content and form are explicitly highlighted. These are embedded within the structure and there are therefore implications for learning within the pretext in terms of knowledge, skills and understanding of drama and theatre form and the chosen content.

The purpose of the pretext is to hook interest, gain commitment, build belief and then gradually to hand over the choice of form and content to the group. There is a movement over the seven or so weeks that the scheme runs from an initial high teacher/low student input in terms of content and form, to high student/low teacher input as the group develops the work. Within the half term's work, a notional seven weeks, all methods of planning and working outlined in 1, 2, 3 and 4 will probably occur.

If the students know that there is the expectation that they will take responsibility for the work after this carefully prepared, quality input, then it can be argued that long term development can take place. In terms of progression this is an important point to make.

Disadvantages

The teacher could dominate the drama in terms of choice of content and form. This could lead students to try to do what 'teacher' wants rather than declare from the start what they would like to develop.

An overview of approaches to planning and working

If the various planning and working methods outlined could be represented in diagrammatic form they would look like this:

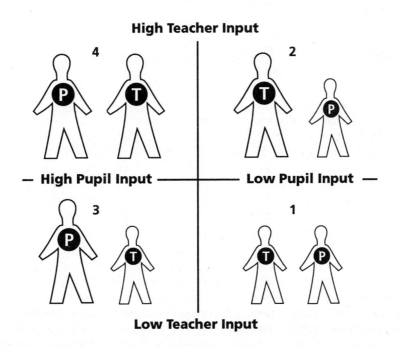

In terms of the development of work from a pretext, the same quadrant diagram illustrates how all the methods of planning and working can best be used within one scheme: there is no pre-determined order.

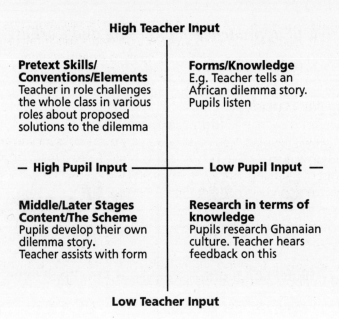

High Teacher Input

**Pretext Skills/
Conventions/Elements**
Teacher in role challenges
the whole class in various
roles about proposed
solutions to the dilemma

Forms/Knowledge
E.g. Teacher tells an
African dilemma story.
Pupils listen

— **High Pupil Input** ——————— **Low Pupil Input** —

**Middle/Later Stages
Content/The Scheme**
Pupils develop their own
dilemma story.
Teacher assists with form

**Research in terms of
knowledge**
Pupils research Ghanaian
culture. Teacher hears
feedback on this

Low Teacher Input

Quality drama teaching, like any other good practice, is encouraged by the movement between all four sections of the quadrant. In drama teaching this is particularly important as it allows the teacher to pace himself in terms of his teaching and the students' learning. In one half term there is a need to move between all four. This approach implies that the intensity of learning has to be managed. The teacher is not a never-ending source of interesting ideas but he does have a clear duty and function to *teach* as well as facilitate.

A drama pretext has no set form in terms of written layout. It is a text that can be read by any practitioner interested in drama and be interpreted according to individual purpose. In this sense it is like any other text, it is not sacrosanct, but does have an integrity, dynamic and aesthetic of its own which has been created through use. It is the scaffolding through which a group's ideas, beliefs, values, attitudes and skills can be explored and presented. It is the pre-text to the group's text.

In this sense it is not simply a very detailed account of a highly successful lesson plan. We have already said that there are implications for learning embedded in pretexts but these cannot all be pre-determined. They are latent within the structure itself.

Just as it would be ludicrous to say that a play is specifically about one thing and one thing only, so it would be unfair to say that a pretext is specifically about one thing only. A good pretext, like a good play, is open to interpretation.

Planning for a pretext

There is no set way to plan. You must find a way that works for you and your group. As you read drama education books you will come across many approaches to the actual lay-out of planning. However, good practice for planning in drama, whatever the lay-out, would usually involve the following:

- clear and simple aims, (drama-specific and general) for a specific group, related directly to needs and wants
- clear and simple learning objectives, in drama-specific and general terms, related to appropriate developmental level
- stimulus and content appropriate for a particular group
- key resources needed for the drama to work
- a point where a contract is made between the teacher and the group and the acknowledgement that it can be re-negotiated
- a clear way of 'getting into' the drama to hook their interest
- key organising questions
- a selection of conventions and tasks that might be used to gain commitment once belief has started to build. These need to be considered carefully from political and ethical angles. It is so easy to reinforce prejudice or bad practice by the way an activity is framed e.g. as regards gender, race, other world cultures, etc.
- a consideration of appropriate ways to involve pupils with special educational needs in the structure of the drama
- a brief outline of possible developments of the drama in future weeks (if appropriate)
- the identification of possible appropriate ways to assess and evaluate the drama, record and if necessary report individual development.

Drama beyond the first session

It is useful to outline briefly possible developments of the drama in 'branch planning' terms. The main planning, however, has to take place in and between each session. As the group become more skilled in handling form (*'I know how we could do that next week!'*) so the planning becomes more of a shared activity.

Planning a drama pretext cannot be approached in a set way but if you keep the points made above in mind, you can plan for drama. In practice you will start your planning at any of the above points and then gradually fill in the rest as the overall structure begins to come clear.

The challenge comes when, for example, the group gives you a subject idea for a drama but neither you nor they can find a way into it. If you are prepared to use your imagination and encourage the group to use theirs, if you are willing to take risks together to find a form for translating ideas into action, then you can plan for drama. You are being creative and the experience could produce a pretext which you craft in hindsight for use with another group in another context.

Starting off

When the time comes to make a start, general ideas are of little use. You need to know 'how' the students get into the drama (form). A big decision to make here is how directly you want to approach the materials. You might feel that you would want initially to approach the subject obliquely. In other words, you might feel that an initial degree of emotional distance between the content and the very real feelings of some of the students is needed. In the long run this could allow the group to face and reflect upon the issues in a more informed way.

You should not feel that you have to have every student in the group up and moving around trying to be someone or do something. You certainly need to hook their interest quickly but this can be done in many ways. You might play a game that begins to focus on the content, you might read a story and ask the class to work on a whole group picture (collective drawing), you might ask them to make a soundtrack for a particular part of the story (sound-tracking), you might show them an object that you have found hidden (artefact).

These are just a few drama conventions that can help you plan the opening frame of the drama and provide a clear task for the students to get involved in. Keep asking yourself, 'What am I asking the students to do at this point?' It may be to listen, watch, imagine, reflect or discuss. Vary these activities by altering the convention (and therefore usually the grouping) to maintain commitment and build belief. An experienced group will know when it is time to change and will also be able to make decisions about an appropriate convention, form or element to switch to or emphasise.

Drama is about 'doing' but the 'doing' itself can be active or passive and in any one lesson there will be times when students are actively in role, moving and speaking from a perspective which is different from their own. But it is unrealistic to ask anyone suddenly to 'be' someone else or to step straight into their shoes or perform for others. They have to be 'protected into the role', just as a play text intended for performance has to be approached carefully through systems of rehearsal. One reason why a lot of people have had embarrassing experiences in drama is that they have not been protected into their roles. They have been asked simply to 'do' without the reassurance of context. We have all heard the stories of people being asked out of the blue to 'be a tree,' or who have been paired up with someone, given a role card to read off and told to start pretending in front of everyone else. No wonder they feel embarrassed!

Once you have hooked the group's interest, you can build the commitment which then establishes belief. This takes time and establishing this context is a part of the process that should not be rushed. The difficult thing is not to take so long over it that the opportunity for drama is lost.

What if things go wrong?

When things go wrong in drama – which they do for all practitioners at times – it can be a painful experience. One reason is that there is nothing for the participants to hide behind. It is clear to everyone involved that the process has ground to a halt. There needs to be re-negotiation on many levels. At the simplest level the leader and the group have to try to agree 'why' things are not working and what a possible way forward might be. Stopping the drama and talking about this is part and parcel of the process. Methods of reflecting on and evaluating the work are built into the pretexts. In our next book *Mapping Drama* we shift the focus from planning to realistic ways of evaluating, assessing, recording and reporting progress in drama. This is intended to offer a framework for reflection – a means to identify perhaps why things have gone wrong in order to increase expertise and confidence through practice.

Drama conventions

As we have already said, a drama convention is a way of organising time, space and action to create meaning. It allows all members of the group to participate in the drama in an organised and creative way. Different conventions also allow for different levels of participation which often means that at one end of the scale individuals can participate and contribute without feeling that they have to do anything embarrassing. At the same time, other individuals can take on a big personal challenge.

A group experienced in drama will be able to suggest conventions that would be useful to develop the drama. It is important to share these terms with the group from their first drama session. In this way they will be able to make suggestions about form as well as content, and will be improving their drama and theatre skills, knowledge and understanding.

The conventions themselves are drawn from a wide range of sources, theatrical, literary, psychological, therapeutic, the arts, etc. They have been in existence for many years. For the purposes of the book, the conventions have been classified into either those used for *Making* or those used for *Reflecting and Evaluating*. These categories are not mutually exclusive. Where a convention is known by a number of names, they have all been given.

Making –

hooking interest, establishing the content, building commitment and developing engagement.

Games:

played together to focus attention, calm down or wake up, to reinforce, or make concrete concepts, to reveal the game structure found in situations, eg. "Tee-ak-ee-allio" in *Gangs* (page 94).

Narrative/voice-over:

commentary/narration: by the leader or a group member over or in front of the action to create atmosphere, give information, help reflection or move the drama on in time, control the action, etc. In its simplest form narration can be used to control the action, e.g. *'The Fairground travellers began slowly to pack away their stalls for the last time.'* in *Rogan's Fair* (page 45)

Supporting sound/sound tracking:

sounds made using voice/body/instruments which are then used to support action. This may be recorded or done live to create atmosphere, consolidate the context, usually used to fit part of the drama, e.g. music for the arrival on the planet in *Space Mission* (page 70).

Hot spot/hot seating:

the group interviews a person in role (the groups may also be in role or not) to build characters, clarify perspectives and the context.

Still images, freeze frame, frozen image, tableaux, set in concrete, photo album:

groups or individuals get into a frozen position which may be looked at, and read, by others to focus closely on one moment or to physically express an abstract concept. The images might be presented as part of the drama as, for example, a photo that has been found, a painting, a sculpture, a statue. This is a very versatile convention and can be used as a form of work in its own right e.g. in *To be or not to be* (page 82) the group form the scene of the murder.

Interviews/interrogations:

in pairs or groups to give or gain information and build roles. Examples include detectives, scientists, TV researchers, barristers, members of a jury, oral history, etc.

Mind parts:

the group are invited to become various parts of a role or character's mind. The conflict within the mind is deconstructed and the various elements within it identified. The group then choose which element they would like to play. The individual playing the role then stands in the middle of these elements. When she points to an element, that group gives all the reasons why she should act as they wish. As soon as she drops her hand, they must fall silent, even in mid sentence. The role can keep on pointing and listening until she feels a decision can be made. This can be a powerful way to build commitment using teacher in role in the middle of the circle, e.g. *To be or not to be* (page 85).

Reconstruction/re-run/re-enactment:

the whole group, or small groups, or pairs carefully reconstruct an incident to explore its dynamics and tensions as in real life crime programmes on TV e.g. 'Crimewatch.' Separate re-enactments could be done from different viewpoints.

Hidden thoughts/speech bubbles/thought-tracking:

one person moves and speaks in role whilst the other speaks the subtext, i.e. what the person is really thinking but cannot say. This helps build roles and reveals dynamics and tensions of the situation. Alternatively, one person can be frozen while the rest of the group are asked if they will individually pass behind this character and speak their thoughts at that particular moment.

TV/radio & newspaper report/coverage/media reports:

events are interpreted or approached through the conventions of TV/radio/ newspaper headlines etc. This can build context by revealing different perspectives, e.g. the finding of the maze in *The Amazing Maze* (page 34).

Mini productions/teams/small group playmaking/improvisation:

the group splits into small groups to demonstrate alternative understandings which may or may not be shared. This can help build roles and situations and can be combined effectively with teacher in role or used as a means of making a statement about the action as performance.

Parallel story/analogy:

the class works as a whole group or in small groups through parallel situations that mirror themes and dynamics in the agreed area to be explored. This requires and encourages objectivity, e.g. *The Rains* (page 109).

Mantle of the expert/the ones who know:

there are various levels at which this convention can be explored. At its simplest, pupils are endowed with specialist knowledge e.g. designers (as in *The Amazing Maze)* or historians. When used in full form, specialist knowledge is not endowed but slowly built through carefully identified tasks which require the gathering of more and more knowledge. This task-driven form of drama builds up strong commitment and belief in roles and situation and can become a form of work in itself.

Simulations:

this emphasises the importance of facts and previously identified dynamics rather than creating drama based on individual and group imagination. Useful in providing background to situation, e.g. if a project on unemployment is producing only stereotypical responses to perceived problems, the drama is shelved for a session and an exercise set up in which the weekly allowance is given to family units, plus a list of their bills. What can they afford to eat that week? A list of current prices is provided. Chance cards with additional financial demands are dropped in, e.g. 'It is one of the family's birthday.' The following session, the group returns to the drama with the insights gained from the simulation.

Defining space:

the action is located in a particular space and defined by an agreed method as the confined space of the squirrel's home in *The Rains* (page 109) is defined by a piece of cloth – a room may be built up with the names of individual features and objects written on small scraps of paper. At its simplest, furniture can be rearranged to represent objects or locations.

Partner-in-role:

another teacher/parent/senior pupil provides the focus for the drama. Information is let out very slowly by the role who carefully listens to contributions by the group and responds to signals from the actual teacher. The group are aware of the person playing the role and may well know them, but that person does not come out of role. The teacher uses the dynamic of the space between the group and the role to create tension as implications are carefully explored. The partnership is between the teacher who is controlling the action and the partner who is acting as the live focus. A partner in role is used simply but effectively in *Space Mission* (page 66).

Costuming:

can be used to hook interest, generate questioning and build belief particularly when used in a partner-in-role situation. The costume itself may be read in a way which begins to suggest a story about the way a person lives, e.g. a simple sword and cloak are used in *To be or not to be* (page 74).

Official messages, letters, diaries, journals, documents:

these can allow movement away from the immediate action of the drama and provide opportunities for the consolidation of individual roles. They can also be used to initiate drama as they provide excellent opportunities for thoughtful, well focused problems to be set in context. They can be written in or out of role. Information technology can be very effective, e.g. taped messages or 'last recordings', photographs, video recordings, word processed documents which could, for example, add authenticity to an official letter, see *Rogan's Fair* (pages 59 & 60) for an example.

Listening in/ eavesdropping/ overheard conversations:

the majority of the group listen to a spontaneous or rehearsed conversation between a pair or smaller group. This provides an opportunity to explore different perceptions of the same event. It can add tension as well as feeding information into the drama.

Drawing maps & diagrams:

a collective activity which can be teacher or group led. It can allow the implications of a particular situation to be carefully explored in visual form at the beginning of, or during the drama, e.g. in *Rogan's Fair* (pages 61 & 62) a plan of the field and scale drawings of the fairground rides are used.

Captions/titles:

a phrase/thought/slogan/graffiti is written large on paper and presented with the action of a particular group. The relationship between the physical action and the written word can have its own resonance, e.g. in *The Amazing Maze*, ten years are spent building a maze (page 37). The group is asked to present a series of images to illustrate this and to give a further insight by giving each image a caption e.g. 'Children are born and grow yet still the work goes on'.

Off-stage pressure:

tension is provided by a force/ power/ person who will soon arrive but is not yet present. This can give impetus to a task which needs completing or a decision which must be made before this arrival, *Space Mission* (page 66) uses this convention.

Role-swap:

at a key moment in the drama, roles are reversed in order to explore the predicament from a totally different perspective.

Forum theatre:

an event/scene is recreated in detail and then replayed. If anyone feels that they would have acted differently at a specific moment within that scene, they put up their hand. The scene is rewound in order for them to step into the action and try their theoretical idea out in practice. The scene can be fast forwarded/slowed down, new characters can be introduced in order to explore the situation. This can be used as form of work in itself.

Artefacts/unfinished materials:

Useful for generating questions to start a piece of drama or to introduce tension during it, e.g. the map in *Rogan's Fair.*

Game shows:

the group agree to explore a difficult issue through a game show format, e.g. in *Rogan's Fair* (page 45) one member of the group could become a game show host. The contestants have to remember what they have seen on a conveyor belt. This is replaced by remembering all the names they have been called, usually as a travelling family. The rest of the group becomes the audience on 'Guess that Prejudice'. The juxtaposition of form and content can be used to start or reflect on a drama.

Teacher-in-role:

a major convention which allows the teacher to challenge, support and develop the drama, and individuals in it, from within the drama. It does not involve the teacher acting but does require conviction and the adoption of an attitude that can be shown in action. Useful in allowing the teacher to encourage the group to see the possibilities of the 'game' of drama.

Telephone talk/long distance communications:

two people speak together with the group as audience. To clarify and control the action, introduce new roles, create tension.

Meetings:

where the space is organised in an agreed way and a procedure established for communication to take place. This allows information to be fed in, problems to be debated, roles clarified and built, e.g. a group of protesters, pirates, police, conspirators, concerned members of the public, or the ride operators in *Rogan's Fair* (page 45).

Collective role:

often at the start of a drama, participants adopt a 'collective role'. For example, they all become astronauts. The emphasis here is often on establishing the situation, focus and perspective through a general role experience. As the drama progresses, participants are encouraged to make these roles more specific or to adopt others in which they see potential, e.g. *Space Mission* (page 66).

Computer input:

an individual, or small group, or the teacher programmes the computer to give an input to the drama. For example, a communication may suddenly start printing out at a moment in the drama which serves to increase tension and focus activity.

Metamorphosis:

the group or individuals can become inanimate objects. This is useful for defining space and giving detail to location. It allows commentary to be made from a different perspective, e.g. *'What would be in the old woman's attic when the students entered? In groups of two or three, find a way of representing a specific object they might find'*.

Reflecting and Evaluating

Drawing together/collective drawing:

the whole group draw on a very large sheet of paper (pieces taped together) or all contribute to it over a period of time, to pool ideas, share perceptions, consolidate the context.

Dance past:

two people are asked to represent the protagonists in a pivotal moment in the drama. The group is then asked if, individually, they would like to take it in turn to model that volunteer into a physical position which they feel literally or abstractly represents their emotional state. When a number of modellings have taken place, the two volunteers are asked to remember the four positions which really captured how this character was feeling.

The group is then split in two and half goes with one volunteer, half with the other. The volunteer then repeats the four physical positionings and then runs them together with link movements to form a short dance/movement phrase. All of the half-group then learns this phrase and practises moving it across the room. When both groups are ready, they stand at opposite sides of the room and rehearse by simply walking the way they will move past each other to get to the opposite side of the room.

After the rehearsal, music and lighting can be added as the two emotions dance past each other. Just before they do this, they are asked to reflect on the feelings and emotions they experience as they dance past the others.

Ceremonial action/rituals & ceremonies:

to show or create a set of repeatable actions, gestures, visual statements that are part of a specific culture or are particular to one person or group of people. They may be devised to honour specific events or may be observable parts of life. These may be rituals of an opening ceremony, e.g. *The Amazing Maze* (page 37).

Marking the moment/where were you?

each person in the drama is asked to go to the exact place where they felt a significant moment occurred for them in the drama. Some of these can be shared or people can be encouraged to reflect on why this was significant for them. A useful way of reflecting on a session or for gathering thoughts when continuing a drama perhaps a week later.

Role-on-the-wall/outline of a person:

draw around a student on a large sheet of paper and use the outline to represent a character in the drama. Facts or characteristics known or perceived are drawn around or in the shape. It can be useful to contrast the outer impressions with the inner truths which are represented so graphically. Individuals can play this collectively agreed-upon figure. This convention features in *To be or not to be* (page 80).

Montage:

selected images, sounds and movements are juxtaposed to evoke feelings and thoughts generated in a drama. Useful in consolidating work or reflecting upon it.

Masks:

can provide a protected way into drama. The making of these allows discussion to take place prior to the action and reduces possible perceived threats. Also a distancing device.

Puppets:

again a safe way into drama work which allows time for discussion during the making process. Also a distancing device.

Empty chair:

place a chair in the centre of a circle. Agree upon and then envisage a chosen character sitting in it. The group asks questions of him/her. The group answers its own questions through the chair, being sensitive to the logic and consistency of the replies.

Two groups-two people:

split the group. One person faces the other whilst the rest of the class stand in two groups (one group behind each individual). The two groups must whisper what they want their individual to say to the other individual. The individual is a mouthpiece for one group. This allows a large group to shape a conversation between two people.

Echo:

the physical setting is the same as 'Two groups – two people', but in this convention the group is the mouthpiece of the individual and can only act as an echo. Useful in building up tension in a conversation between two people which actually involves a whole group. To add tension, the individuals and the groups can physically move towards each other during the conversation. The two individuals at the front of each group lead the speeches which must be in short phrases or sentences to work.

Song:

taped or sung live, this can be used to complement or provide a contrast to action or to reflect on or in a drama, e.g. songs could be written in groups to commemorate key moments in the history of the maze in *The Amazing Maze* (page 34).

Sculpture:

one person models an image by physically manipulating an individual or group of individuals. Useful in exploring individual perceptions and can be developed by subsequently exploring 'ideal' images and the realistic possibilities of transition between them and those first created. Much of the value of this convention lies in the rest of the group reading the image, i.e. saying what information and/or feeling this gives them.

Tunnel of decision/conscience corridor/conscience alley:

the group form two parallel lines and try to verbally influence the decision of the individual who walks down the alley between them. By the time the individual reaches the end of the alley/corridor, she or he must have decided on a course of action in response to arguments /chants/ pleas. Useful in consolidating individuals' decisions, thoughts and feelings.

Either/or:

ask the group to choose between two options which in effect divide the class in half, e.g. *'If you think you would rush and get help, sit on the right of the room. If you think you would attempt a rescue yourself, sit on the left.'* This is useful for managing the drama and creating two audiences. Most importantly, it gives the group the opportunity to see that they can determine the direction of the drama. This has to be true, as they all may decide to sit on one side of the room and developments accordingly take place from there. This convention is used to influence the outcome in *The Rains* (page 114).

Continuum:

draw an imaginary line down the centre of the room and place the word 'Yes' at one end of the room and 'No' at the opposite. Place a chair to the side of the room at mid point on the continuum. Ask anyone who wants to, to stand on the chair and ask any question relating to a character or issue that they would like to ask. The rest of the group must then move to yes or no or some point in between on the continuum.

This is a useful way to allow individuals to make statements without having to defend them verbally. It allows the group to see physically and visually that there are many differences of opinion in a group, e.g. in *The Rains* (page 109) *'Do you think that animals are better companions than humans?'*

Moving sculpture/essence machine:

one person is invited to walk into the centre of the room and start repeating a small piece of movement (with repeated words or sounds). One by one, the others join in this moving and audible sculpture. This convention can move responses away from the literal to the abstract and conceptual.

Mime:

individuals or small groups communicate with the rest of the group using their body rather than words. This can encourage participation for those who feel unsure of speaking e.g. when choosing roles in a group of Elizabethan travelling players, each person mimes what they do, (juggle etc) and the rest of the group quickly guess. Mime is used to establish identities and atmosphere in *To be or not to be* (page 77).

If you find yourself using a particular structuring technique in drama, add your own convention to the list, but remember that planning a pretext requires more thought than simply listing a string of conventions.

Introduction to the Pretexts

These schemes of work can be used with all ages and abilities. We realise this is quite a claim, but we stick by it. They have developed from initial ideas through years of trial and error into their present form. You will, of course, change and develop them, improving them into pretexts that work for you.

The Aims and Learning Outcomes given for each pretext are examples only.

We have not specified cross-curricular links in all cases, but they are there within all of the pretexts. A full example is given in *Rogan's Fair* (page 52-56).

Each pretext is printed in two forms. Firstly, as a narrative which outlines the drama in detail. Within this form the teacher's instructions to the group are presented as a script like this:

> We are going to start today
> with a game called 'Cat and
> Mouse'.

The intervening directions are presented like this:

> Group to stand in five or six parallel rows with
> their arms extended.

The conventions used are shown in boxes in the margin. Secondly the pretext is given in grid form for quick reference or to reflect upon and deconstruct a session. This highlights the reasons behind steps taken and suggests where a particular emphasis should be given to sustain the drama.

Timings for activities have been left largely up to the discretion of teachers. You will know your group best and may well need to be flexible anyway. A short amount of time can, on one occasion, focus thoughts and ensure quality work whilst on others it produces only a superficial response. Similarly, a longer time span can, on one occasion, lead to lack of purpose and direction whilst, on another, can allow in-depth, thoughtful, quality work to emerge. When our experience in running the pretext tells us an activity usually does benefit from a particular time limit, we have broken the rule and presumed to give one.

The overall amount of time spent working with a group on a pretext is also left up to the individual practitioner. We have used pretexts occasionally as one-off sessions but usually employ them as a basis and an essential structure for a full half term's work or project. As has often been said in drama education, quality work comes not from having dozens of bright ideas, but rather from one good idea, carefully developed.

The Amazing Maze

Used with lower and upper Primary, Secondary, 16+, Undergraduates, PGCE, In-Service and community groups.

Aim

to engage the group in a cross-curricular drama project, focusing particularly on history, mathematics, technology and English.

Learning Outcomes

Drama Skills /Knowledge	Social Skills	Possible Learning Areas
Use language appropriate to context	Work constructively in various groupings	Information on mazes and labyrinths, religious and historical roots
Adopt, sustain and develop a role	Accept other people's ideas and work with them	Mathematical basis of mazes e.g. multicursal & unicursal, six steps to a classical maze – design & technology
Be responsible for more than one role	Present ideas in a formal setting	
Use gesture appropriate to context		Understanding that historical 'facts' are often 'perceptions'
		The transience of human achievement
		Environmental awareness related to technological development

GAME

We are going to start today with a game called 'Cat and Mouse'.

Group to stand in five or six parallel rows with their arms extended.

When I say turn, you all turn to your right. We need a volunteer to be the Cat and one to be the Mouse. The Cat has to tig the Mouse. You have to go down the rows, you cannot pass through people's arms.

Let several couples have a go.

Next time do the same, only the Cat and Mouse have to close their eyes. The rest of the group have to make sure no harm comes to them.

Third time (with new volunteers) as the Cat and Mouse pass you, make comments or sounds which may unsettle them. For instance,

You'll never get out. You are lost forever.

Let everyone have a go.

DISCUSSION

What did it feel like? Has anyone ever been lost in a maze? What do you think it would be like to be lost in a maze?

NARRATION

We'll start the drama now. Would you come and sit around me and listen to a story.

Once upon a long ago there lived a King and Queen in a far away land.

As a group can we now build up a picture of what that land looked like?

Questions like:

Were there any mountains?

Was the Palace on a hill?'

What were the King and Queen like?

One day the King called for his Queen. He was restless and unhappy. He knew that one day he would die, but he wanted to be remembered. He didn't want a statue like everyone else. And then it came to him. He would have a maze built in his honour. A maze that would last forever. An amazing maze that would mean he would never be forgotten. He called together teams of the best architects, builders, gardeners, artists and mathematicians in the world and told them of his decision.

Thank you for coming here today, you are the best designers and builders in the known world. You have one month in which to design a maze in my honour. A maze that will last forever. Money is no object. The best design will be chosen, and the designers rewarded with wealth beyond their wildest dreams. The losers will get nothing. Go now, and return in one month.

GROUP PLANNING

Get into groups of three to six.

You are a design team. Go away now and design a maze, you have plenty of time so don't rush. The resources are over here (sugar paper, felt tips, templates etc.). There are also some sheets here to give you some ideas. Share the background information with the group. If you can do some research of your own, that may be very useful.

At the end you will have to present your designs. Off you go.

PRESENT THE DIAGRAM	Towards the end of the planning process, feed in the need for a quality presentation, and discuss the skills necessary e.g. clear diction, everyone to say something, use of visual aids like the designs, etc.
TEACHER IN ROLE (KING)	Thank you very much, next one please. Collect them in as you go along. Thank you very much for all of your efforts. I have considered them all carefully and have decided to take the best bits from each and design one myself. You will all be rewarded, thank you so much.
NARRATION	Once the King had finalised his design, the builders sprang into action. It was to take 10 years to complete.
STILL IMAGES	In groups of four to eight could you do a series of images which show the maze being built? Maybe you could do one for each of the ten years. We'll show them as if they were a slide show – with three seconds between each one. This means you'll have to rehearse moving from one to the next.
CAPTION	You might want to give each one a caption. Show and discuss.
NARRATION	After 10 years of hard toil, the maze was complete. The King and Queen were so delighted with the result that they decided to have a special ceremony to celebrate the opening of the maze.
CEREMONY	In groups of five to ten, devise a ceremony to celebrate the opening of the maze.

Suggest use of speeches, movement, dances, responses, music, entertainment, food, etc.

NARRATION

The King and Queen grew older and, as is the way of things, they died. The years flew past and many changes came to the country. The Palace fell into ruin and a forest began to grow around the maze and over the whole land. Eventually the maze was visited no more. However, it was not forgotten and many stories about it were told. These were passed down from generation to generation.

STORYTELLING /LEGEND

In groups of three to six devise and present a story about the maze.

Show and discuss.

NARRATION

After thousands of years, the maze had been totally forgotten by everyone. Safe in the middle of an impenetrable rainforest, its secrets seemed safe forever. However, earlier this year, a logging company was stripping a forest of its hardwoods, when the workers stumbled upon the entrance to the maze. The workers thought they heard the noises of people living inside. Within hours, the world's press gathered.

NEWS REPORT

In groups of three to four, present a news report on the finding of the maze. Each group must do it in a certain style.

Give each group the choice of:

a) Reporter for BBC news
b) Children's news item
c) A soap opera
d) A rap artist

Branch Planning

Split the group in half or into three or four groups depending upon the size.

Tasks

1. Decide on another group of people with whom you might choose to work – usually a younger group.

2. Each half is to plan a drama education session for this target group. You are to be people who live in a section of the maze. The target group are the explorers who come into the maze.

The Amazing Maze

	Step	Reason	Convention	Emphasis
1	Game of Cat and Mouse	To experience some of the fun and fear of being in a maze	Game	Keep it safe and controlled
2	Discussion about Cat & Mouse	To begin to clarify feelings about mazes and information	Discussion Not in role	The way mazes affect feelings once inside
3	Narrate the opening of the story telling of the King's decision to build a maze as a memorial	Establish the context for the action. Give groups a common focus	Narration	The class are in role as the best in their profession. The maze must immortalise the King & Queen
4	As the King, encourage imagination to be used in the designs. Ask them to return in one month	To clarify the task and give insights into the King's character	Teacher in role Mantle of the expert	Money is no problem
5	In groups, design a maze using materials provided	A task driven section of the drama to allow the expertise of the designers, etc to be established & grow	Small group work. Teacher in role	Encourage the groups to keep their work secret. Involve and challenge as the King, or gently support their work
6	Groups present their designs to the King	Language demands are made on the group as they try to convey the often complex and symbolic ideas & concepts that lie behind their designs	Teacher in role with small groups in forum	Encourage sycophancy to the King
7	Narrate the passing of 10 years & ask for a series of still images for the King	To shift & reframe the drama	Narration Caption	Three seconds between each photo

Step	Reason	Convention	Emphasis
8 Discuss the images/ photography as they are shown by the group	To see if the group are engaging with other levels of the drama such as that of the wish to have 'our' name last through time	Discussion Still Image	Explore the resonance (or not) between image and caption
9 Narration of the opening ceremony which has to be devised	To move into other forms of work in drama, music and movement to vary the pace of the session	Narration & ceremony	Groups of five to ten that will be linked by the teacher
10 Narrate the passing of time and disrepair of the maze. Present the story of the maze as a devised piece of theatre	To reframe the drama, to show that history is often not made up of facts but perceptions	Narration/Storytelling Small group playmaking	Keep the story or legend simple, even conversational
11 Narrate the maze being forgotten and discovered in the present day. The world's press gather	To reframe the drama	Narration	Allow for a discussion of how places are lost in time and then rediscovered
12 News report of the present day findings in the various forms a) By a current newsreader (e.g. Kate Adie) b) Children's news (e.g. Blue Peter) c) A soap opera d) A rap artist	To reframe the drama	Song, report from the media	Maintain the given style either a, b, c or d

Background information on mazes

Mazes and labyrinths have their origins in religious beliefs and can be traced back thousands of years in time. There are maze patterns drawn on the side of pots and coins from the Greek and Roman civilisations. Maiden Castle in Dorset has been found to have maze type outer defence walls. It was first built in 350 BC, in the Iron Age, as a fort. Today many mazes can be found in the large country houses of England. The most famous is probably Hampton Court maze. Most people are likely to come across them at places like Blackpool Pleasure Beach where there are two mazes. One is an outdoor maze and is made of hedges with a tower in the middle. The other is indoors and is made of glass and mirrors. Some travelling fairs have mirror and glass mazes on trailers. In the past, mazes have been made from a wide variety of materials.

Many myths and legends have been passed through the ages about mazes and they have a tremendous hold on the imagination. Crete is the location for one of the most famous labyrinth legends. This was the home of the Minoans. At the centre of this labyrinth dwelled the Minotaur who was half man and half bull. Every few years, seven young men and women were sent from Athens into the labyrinth and never seen again. Theseus, who was from Athens, found a way to retrace his footsteps from the labyrinth.

The word 'labyrinth' may have originated from the name of the Minoan double headed axe – 'labrys'.

There are many ways to design a maze. Some of the oldest are based on the classical, seven circle design. Mathematical formulae can be used to construct very challenging designs. There are two main categories of design. Unicursal means there is only one entrance and way to the centre. Multicursal means there is more than one entrance and more than one way to get to the centre.

Some mazes have traps, tricks and tests of ingenuity on the way to the centre. What is in the centre is always the reason for trying so hard to get there. Sometimes it is just the reward of looking back down upon the way you have come and the 'pleasure' of seeing other people lost and frustrated. Sometimes there is something of incredible beauty or power at the centre. The difficulty is always how to get out again without getting lost – perhaps for ever.

Recommended books:
Fisher, A. & Sayward J. 1993 *The British Maze Guide* Minotaur Designs
Fisher, A. & Gerster G 1991 *The Art of the Maze* Weidenfield and Nicholson
Bord, J. 1989 *Mazes and Labyrinths of the World* Latimer New Dimensions

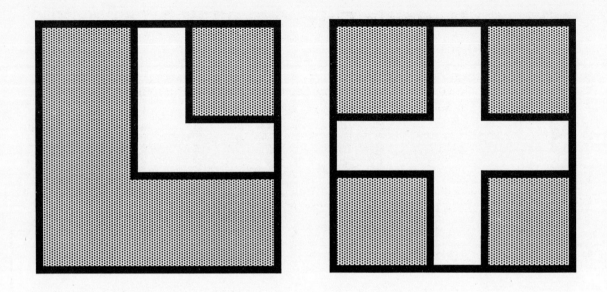

Rogan's Fair

Used with Upper Primary, Secondary,16+, Undergraduates, PGCE, In-Service and community groups.

Aim

to explore the culture of the 'traveller' in society. Initially this is through a dramatised real life mathematical problem.

Learning outcomes

Drama Skills/Knowledge	Social Skills	Possible Learning Areas
Adopt, sustain and develop a number of roles	Problem solving Empathy	Multicultural, Travellers, Romanies, Gypsies, Tinkers, etc.
Interact in role. Add to the whole drama whilst creating individual roles	Use a range of language registers appropriate to context	Mathematics – interpreting data – number, shape and space
Reverse roles with commitment and belief		Citizenship Prejudice
Call upon a range of subtle skills in voice and movement to sustain and develop dramatic action		
Select own material for dramatic work and sense that it has potential		

Resources

Seven site plans (page 61), seven scale outlines of all the fairground rides and stalls (page 62) one cut up in each of the seven envelopes numbered with the name of the ride on it. (You may wish to photocopy these A4 size or larger for ease of handling). Letter from the Safety Board (page 59), letter from Farmer Higson (page 60), seven sets of: tables of figures for this year's predicted financial takings (page 63), the last ten years' takings (page 64), charts (page 65) showing relation of ground space to income generated. Material on Travellers to be introduced as appropriate. Ideas for this are given in the branch planning section.

THE CONTRACT

The project you are going to start is about a travelling fair. It is based on a story about one fair called Rogan's Fair, which is quite a small outfit. I am going to control the start of the drama quite tightly but then you will be able to develop it.

If agreement is reached then the group move quickly into the next activity.

Stand in a circle. Will each of you start thinking about travelling fairs. I am going to set you a challenge: Can the whole group think of forty rides or stalls that could be found on a fair? I will count.

Give a few moments for individuals to think of some rides, then give the option of sharing ideas with a partner.

Watch me and see if you can quickly guess the ride I have thought of.

Mime this e.g. firing a rifle on the rifle range. Then ask the class to help guess all the rides that are mimed as they work their way around the circle.

The aim is to think of as many rides as possible as a whole group. If anyone's mind goes blank, or if anyone uses a ride someone else was thinking of, that person can just say 'Pass' and will get another chance to contribute the next time it is their turn in the circle.

Start the activity and support all contributions, encouraging cross-circle talk about rides that you sense excite the group.

This is a quick step into action which is non-threatening as it allows individuals to be involved without putting them on the spot. The number challenge is important as it puts the focus on the group's achievement which is something everyone can share in.

This activity also shows the class that they have a considerable knowledge about fairs and that their ideas are valued.

We are going to start the story soon but before we do, it is important to sort out some basic things.

**STARTING
THE DRAMA
ADOPTING
ROLES**

Firstly let us sort out who is running what ride on this small travelling fair.

Go round the circle and split the group into seven groups. As each group is identified, give the name of the ride it runs. These are:

THE HAUNTED HOUSE   THE ARCADE   THE WALTZER

MINI DODGEMS   BIG WHEEL   HAMBURGER STAND

THE RIFLE RANGE

A strong group should be chosen for the Haunted House as the drama focuses strongly on them initially.

To start with I will be the SITE MASTER for Rogan's Fair. In other words I am the person who sorts out all the arrangements to do with the fairground sites.

This involves fixing a site plan for each new site which shows exactly where each ride is to be situated and just how much room it can have. It also involves dealing with the site owners and all the other administrative business of the fair.

I know where and when the story starts.

It starts in a field on the last-site-but-one of the season. Rogan's Fair is packing up ready to leave for the last site which is the best in the year. On this site we usually make enough money to see us through the winter months on our winter sites. This is the time when rides and stalls are repaired, repainted and made ready for the new year's work. It is ten minutes to go before the fair moves on. The wagons and lorries have been loaded and the last bolts are being fastened, the last ropes tied and the last safety checks being made before going on the road. All the talk is of the next six days' work and the hopes for a winter rest.

Ask the groups to move to a place in the room where their lorry or wagon is located. When they are in position, ask:

Can the story start? This is going to be a challenge as everyone is going to pretend to be a member of the fair as they make their final preparations for the road. Try to keep the drama going for five minutes. During that time I will also be the Site Master and may well talk to you as that character as you mime the final preparations, perhaps talking back as you do so.

We have now established:

Your ROLES (who you will pretend to be for the purposes of the drama i.e. you will become fairground ride owners as agreed and I will be the Site Master).

The LOCATION (the setting in which the drama takes place i.e. last but one site of the year).

The ACTION (the activity happening at the very moment the drama starts i.e. loading the lorries and making final checks before travelling).

The PERSPECTIVE (the viewpoint from which we are coming to step into the action i.e. hard working people looking forward to a rest and to repairing equipment on the winter site).

Okay – let's start.

Having started the drama it is essential to demonstrate the level of commitment and belief expected from the group.The group will quickly pick up these signals from your voice and movement and use these as models for their own contribution.

When the five minutes come to an end, you as the Site Master call everyone together and ask them to come to your booth.

You have probably been wondering why I have not packed away. The reason is that there is a problem with the next site. A letter has come from the Safety Inspector. Without any warning, at the very end of a busy season, new regulations have been introduced. A new compulsory distance between rides has been introduced together with some other minor regulations. This is as a result of a number of accidents caused earlier in the year by overcrowding sites with rides and stalls.

Read the letter out loud (page 59)

I have been trying to see how on earth all the rides can fit on to the last site in the light of the new regulations.

(Produce the other letter. See page 60).

Unfortunately I have more bad news. It is from the owner of Higson's Field, the field we always use as the last site of the year. I will read his letter to you.

Can you see a way of fitting everyone in to Higson's Field without breaking the new two metre rules?

Each fairground ride or stall group is given a scale plan of the field (see Higson's Field, page 61), scaled outlines of each ride or stall's shape (see Rides, page 62) and a scaled paper ruler (see Rides, page 62).

I suggest we all meet back in ten minutes to see if any one has found a way of fitting all the rides into the field. We need to be on the road soon or it will be dark when we arrive at Higson's Field. If this is the case we will not be able to set the rides and stalls up for tomorrow's business and we will all lose much needed money.

SMALL GROUP
PROBLEM
SOLVING
IN OR OUT
OF ROLE

Using real letters in the drama helps to focus attention and builds belief. In this case they set the parameters of the drama and generate action and the tension needed for the drama to progress i.e. the new regulations mean that all the rides cannot fit into the field unless one or two gaps are slightly less than two metres or one of the rides drops out. Both are difficult decisions to make. If the regulations are broken and there is a safety inspection or someone gets injured, everyone will be held responsible in law and will have this on their conscience. If a ride or stall drops out then that group of people will not have enough money to see them through the winter months.

There is no possibility of using another field as Mr Higson the farmer has already told them about the saplings he has planted. There is no possibility of finding another site at such short notice as the rest of the village do not seem to want the fair anyway. Even if a field was found, they are obliged to Mr Higson and this site has been advertised.

<table>
<tr><td>

WHOLE
GROUP
ROLE PLAY

</td></tr>
</table>

As the groups work on the problem, the Site Master converses in role. He reinforces the points contained in the letters and previous drama.

Call everyone together.

> Has anyone managed to solve the problem?

Look at the plans. Be honest in pointing out where regulations have been compromised. The fact becomes clear that unless regulations are broken, even in a minor way, all the rides will not fit in the field. Offer a real alternative here of taking the risk and all squeezing on, but make it clear that everyone will be responsible. Before this decision is taken, introduce some more material: figures showing how much each ride and stall should have made this year and how much they charged (page 63).

As the Site Master, at the appropriate moment remark very coolly that the HAUNTED HOUSE has again taken very little money, charges the highest prices and takes up the most space.

> I told you at the time that welding that huge extension
> on was a mistake. Always in your family no one listens
> to reason.

Let discussion take place about this.

You are really, as teacher, highlighting that at the heart of this problem are people and whatever decision is taken involves them. You are also pointing out that the figures being discussed could help the group to take a decision. In putting pressure on the HAUNTED HOUSE group you are opening up the dynamics of this group of people. You will be watching to see if anyone else defends this ride or if the other workers start to join in criticism having realised that this may prevent their ride from leaving the fair on Higson's Field. Encourage the discussion of the figures.

As the Site Master, introduce another set of figures (page 64) which outlines the money each ride has taken every year for the last ten years. Once again point to the poor takings, high charges and large ground space of the HAUNTED HOUSE. Discussion in role continues.

As the teacher, you are encouraging the pupils to explore the figures to provide some sort of answer to their problem. The ten year figures contain some interesting information. Why for example did takings from the HAUNTED HOUSE suddenly go up several years ago and then remain at that level? Why has the ARCADE always done so well over the years? etc.

As the Site Master, introduce more information about ground space taken up by each ride in comparison with takings and ride charges. This is in the form of graphs (page 65). Discussion continues.

As the teacher, you are encouraging the group to look at the issues the figures are raising in graphic terms. More material for dialogue in the drama is being generated. The problem is becoming more urgent as time is passing and a start must be made on the journey to Higson's Field. This is not a simple balloon debate as the consequences to each decision will have to be lived with in the drama.

Branch Planning

Many choices are now available in the drama. At the beginning of this work, as the teacher, you tell the group that you know the story up to a particular point but no further. You could well stop the drama now and let the group know that this point has been reached. Whatever choices they make now will determine the way the drama develops.

This is a crucial stage in the project. It marks the point between the non-negotiable drama structure and the negotiable form about to begin. You can now capitalise on the motivation, enthusiasm and understanding generated through the initial structure. Hopefully you will use this commitment and belief to enter other learning areas.

The group may have already made it apparent which choice they favour. More likely than not there will be several choices under consideration. You now have to help the group explore the avenues and issues which are important to them. Whether or not you choose to follow these developments will depend upon the constraints or freedom of the curriculum in which you operate. For example:

- Other financial arrangements could be made to support the one ride which does not go on to Higson's Field e.g. each ride could give a percentage of their takings or an agreed sum of money, or an agreed sum of money related to income to the excluded ride. Another alternative could be to charge one overall admittance price and pay the excluded ride out of these takings etc. Each of these arrangements would of course need working out from figures used in the project to date. This could lead to much work in Mathematics and use of Information Technology, perhaps a computer for handling data. Such work could be done in the course of the week. The personal implications of the figures could then be explored in role in another drama session in the following week (for example, if a general percentage of each ride's takings were to be given to the excluded ride would it not be unfair for the ARCADE who would lose a great deal more than the BIG WHEEL? Or should ability to pay be related to income?) Work is also focusing here on the basic Economic Awareness needed to run a small business as part of a larger corporation.

- The group might want to take a risk and break the regulations, even if 'only slightly.' If this line is taken, the implications of this decision could be followed through and teased out, e.g. the Safety Inspector Mr Toft could arrive just as the fair is about to open, or there could be an accident as a result of the regulations being broken. This could result in a prosecution and court case. Many aspects of Health and Safety Education will be explored here e.g. a consideration of the practicalities and problems of introducing safety rules that will actually be adhered to. If this line is followed, there will also be much scope for work in English. Speaking and listening skills are obviously central to the whole drama process. This option would also introduce many different contexts for language use e.g. if the accident line is taken, the incident may best be presented in the form of a short newsflash on local or national radio. This would require the group to consider an appropriate language register.

- Likewise the accident option may lead to the use of a formal language register in the preparation of statements and testimonies. The whole of the story about Rogan's Fair could be used as the basis for a creative piece of writing. The shared drama framework could provide a useful structure for an individually shaped story. Appropriate parts of the drama could be scripted either to further the exploration, to reflect upon it or to consolidate it. The accident option would also allow for science work. Out of the drama, the group could decide what exactly went wrong e.g. there could be a fire as a result of an electrical fault or a more serious accident as a result of metal fatigue on one of the rides. Both these examples have a basis in reality and in the logic of the drama e.g. in relation to the safety regulations.

- The group may enjoy building their rides and stalls to make the drama clearer. Work in Technology could be very productive here. The need to design their ride will have been clearly identified in terms of the drama. They could generate a design based on the limited information given. This could be realised in a working model and evaluated not only in terms of design but in terms of the drama as well e.g. why is the HAUNTED HOUSE so big yet so unpopular?

- The class might be interested in finding out more about travelling fairs. This could lead on to work in Art. Fairground design is a unique form of work with a rich history. This form moves from elaborate sign painting to creative pieces of work done by specialists and the ride owners themselves. Each group could paint their own designs or works of 'fair art.' This could be done in various media either on an agreed model of the ride or totally separate from it.

- Interest in fairs could lead in to work in Music. Again there is a rich history of this. Traditional and modern music played at fairs could be explored. A tape could be made that genuinely reflected the sort of music played at fairs. It could include other sound arrangements which would add to the atmosphere of the fair in the drama.

- The group might decide that one of the rides is simply excluded from Higson's Field or they might decide to try to persuade someone else in the village to make a bigger field available. If any such decision is made, it will mean that either a small group or the whole group as fair workers will have to deal with other members of the public. This can lead to work in Citizenship, e.g. what are the rights and responsibilities of the individual in society, particularly when they choose, or are born into, an alternative lifestyle to those lived by the majority of the population? This will offer opportunities to look at the multicultural dimensions of this work, e.g. the rich culture of the Romany way of life could be explored. The Romany language could be investigated and the nature of their seasonal way of life compared to the majority who live in fixed housing. The many different types of travellers could also be explored e.g. tinkers, Romanies etc.

- This could also lead in to work in Equal Opportunities e.g. what rights do travellers have in education, health care, sites to live on and job opportunities? All of these cross curricular elements and dimensions could be explored in the drama e.g. the ride workers that have been excluded try to find other work. What kind of response do they get? e.g.the fair workers approach other members of the community in the search for a larger site. What type of response do they meet? etc.

- Work in History and Geography might be appropriate if the group want to find out more about past problems travellers have faced e.g. personal accounts from travellers could be used to inform action in the drama. This could bring in information on the way travellers are treated in different countries and have been treated in different periods of history e.g. victims of the Nazis in Hitler's Germany and of the Stalinist regime in the USSR (travelling homes were cemented to the ground on permanent sites in this last case). Tracing the history of travelling people will lead the group all over the world. Numerous stories of the origin of the 'original gypsies' abound; e.g. when one of the great pharaohs had no more use for the workers who had built one of the great pyramids he turned them away. So much time had passed since they left their homeland of Persia that they could not return and so set out to roam the world.

All of the above choices and many more are open to the group. You may want to lead them through all of these areas. The drama itself may take many forms depending on decisions taken within the overall story. The teacher's task is to try to match form to content and feeling e.g. a radio news flash of an accident on the fair might deepen the belief in the drama rather than trying to reconstruct it so the teacher may decide to swap roles and play the Safety Inspector Mr Toft, who suddenly arrives just as the fair is about to open. This might secure a deeper response than asking the groups to go away separately and work on what might happen. The teacher using drama has to think as quickly as the students and continually make choices about the form or convention of drama most appropriate for a given purpose.

Rogan's Fair

Step	Reason	Convention	Emphasis
1 Establish the contract. This drama has a very structured start but its direction depends upon group decisions. It's about a travelling fairground initially	To let the group know that all of the drama will not be as tightly controlled as the first section	Contract	The drama will involve mathematics but this should be interesting material for the drama
2 In a circle, mime as many travelling fairground rides and stalls as the group knows. The rest of the group guess the mime. If any individual can't think of one they say 'pass'	Begins to introduce the group's knowledge of fairgrounds	Game, mime	Keep it moving quickly, keep going round the circle
3 Split the group into seven groups. Distribute envelopes with the names of their ride/stall on and ask them not to open it yet. Teacher as Site Master	Quickly gives a role and adds the interest of what is in the envelope	Adopting roles	Choose a strong/able group for the Haunted House
4 Establish the location: they are packing up on the penultimate site to move to the last site. Establish action: making the last adjustments to lorries etc. Establish the perspective: hard working people looking forward to making enough money on the last pitch to see them through the winter	Allows the group the chance to quickly move into a clearly defined context	Whole group role play	As Site Master, join in the packing away and converse in role. e.g. 'How did you go on last night?'

Step	Reason	Convention	Emphasis
5 There has been a new regulation from the safety board. How can all the rides/ stalls fit on the last site when the distance between them has been increased?	Establishes the focus. Sets the problem	Meeting	Produce the safety board letter. Let the group know you have been working hard but can find no solution
6 Introduce a scale map for each group and ask if they can solve this. Scale plans of their rides are in the envelopes they already have	There is no way to do this without compromising safety or without a ride leaving. This has obvious implications for the drama and introduces tension	Small group problem solving in or out of role	Let them know there may be a way. Maybe you are just too tired to see it?
7 Call the groups together and carefully look at possible physical solutions	To respect their effort	Whole group role play	Make it clear that they have worked well but either compromising safety or one leaving may be the only alternative
8 As the discussion in role progresses, hand out the figures you have for the takings, say that you think they 'tell a story'. As you hand out the last 10 years' figures and graphs, begin to add tension by letting the group know it is getting late and you should really be going	The implications in the figures suggest alternative directions in the drama	Prepared materials introduced to whole group role play	Drop into the conversation that 'if only the Haunted House had not had its extension welded on, the problem could easily be solved'
9 Stop the drama and ask the group if there are any acceptable mathematical solutions to the problem	Pulls away from the role play to allow a decision about the direction of the drama	Discussion	Let the group know that from this point the drama explores the directions they are interested in

British
Fair Safety Board

1 Bedford Way, Sheffield S10 39B
Tel: 0114 2743282

Dear Site Master,

You are hereby informed of new Health and Safety Legislation relating to the running and organisation of travelling fairgrounds.

1. There shall be a minimum spacing between each unit of 2 metres. (A unit being defined as any ride, stall or booth in the fairground area).

2. The Site Master's Booth must be located within the fairground itself. As well as being a centre for the public to readily seek information, it should also serve as a base for first aid.

3. All generators should be located within the ride's allotted site space.

4. All cables should be covered with a heavy duty P.F.C. capping.

This legislation is now in effect. Any transgression will result in the prosecution of each and every listed member of the fair.

Yours sincerely,

A Toft

(A. Toft – Inspector).

Oaktree Farm
Little Hampton
01461 4889

Dear Mr Rogan,

In reply to your letter of last month, I must let you know that only Higson's Field is going to be open for use again this year. We have planted saplings in the surrounding fields and do not want these to be damaged in any way. You can park your vehicles as usual in the small paddock up near the farm.

You should also know that we have been put under a lot of pressure by our neighbours and people in the village not to let you on. However in the light of our past arrangements we have decided that the fair should go ahead this year anyway.

Hope things are all right with you all.

J Higson

Jack Higson.

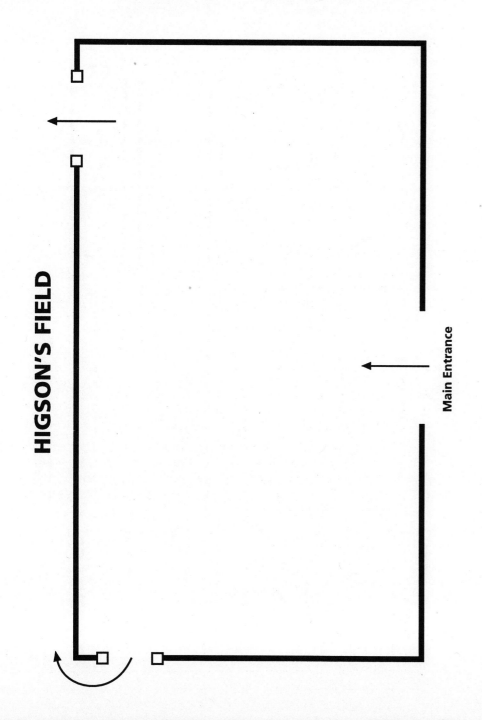

HIGSON'S FIELD

Main Entrance

RIDES

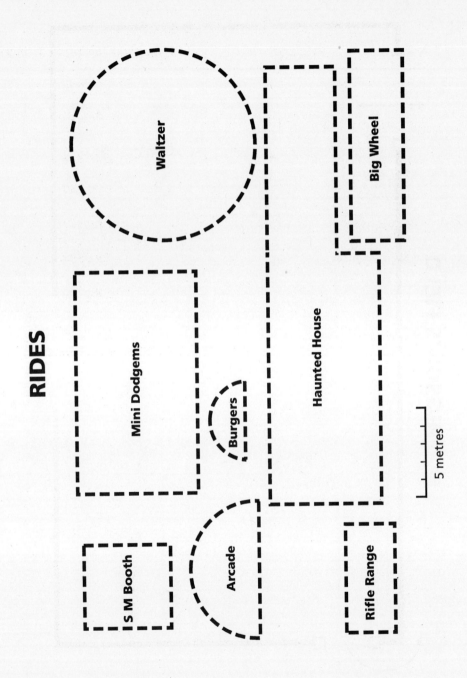

Waltzer

Big Wheel

Mini Dodgems

Burgers

Haunted House

Arcade

S M Booth

Rifle Range

5 metres

Name	Price per ride	Predicted takings – This year
Arcade	—	£26, 020
Waltzer	£1	£21, 590
Big Wheel	80p	£18, 324
Rifle Range	60p	£18, 250
Haunted House	£1.25	£13, 880
Mini Dodgems	80p	£20, 584
Burger Bar	—	£18, 100
TOTAL TAKINGS		£136, 748

Declared takings for the last 10 years											
	1	2	3	4	5	6	7	8	9	10	*Pred.
Arcade	15,100	15,950	16,720	17,030	16,900	17,660	18,000	19,100	21,027	24,050	26,020
Waltzer	9,260	10,057	10,518	9,171	10,600	11,721	11,940	13,871	15,150	19,590	21,590
Big Wheel	9,010	9,271	9,876	9,111	9,010	9,720	9,013	11,720	13,158	16,324	18,324
Rifle Range	5,871	5,971	6,700	6,950	7,100	7,895	8,000	11,120	13,100	16,851	18,250
Haunted House	5,840	5,412	5,002	4,841	4,807	4,111	4,030	3,950	8,059	10,524	13,880
Mini Dodgems	7,150	7,990	8,000	8,580	8,900	9,014	9,860	13,600	15,000	19,143	20,584
Burger Bar	6,780	6,500	6,590	6,887	7,521	8,000	8,190	11,010	11,143	16,642	18,100

*Predicted

HAUNTED HOUSE: TAKINGS FOR THE LAST 10 YEARS

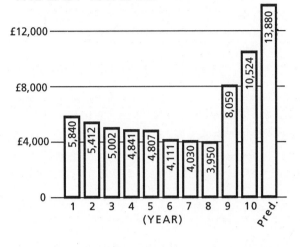

MONEY TAKEN BY EACH RIDE THIS YEAR (Approx)

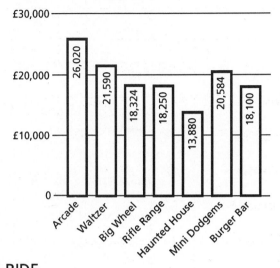

GROUNDSPACE USED BY EACH RIDE

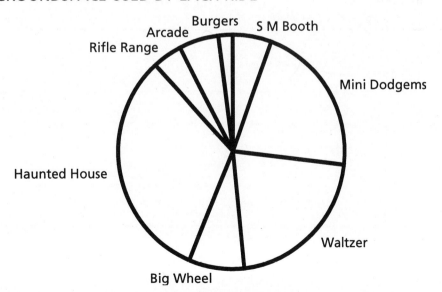

Space Mission

Used with Upper Primary, Secondary, 16+, Undergraduates, PGCE, In-Service.

Aim

to engage the group in a drama which will quickly allow them to work together in order to come to a decision.

Learning Outcomes

Drama Skills/Knowledge	Social Skills	Possible Learning Areas
Demonstrate a knowledge of symbol and metaphor	Co-operation	Promises
	Teamwork	Other cultures
Develop appropriate drama forms	Decision making	Environmental issues
Develop convincing roles		

Resources

Tape player, stirring music for viewing the planet, stick-on labels made into badges, envelope containing orders.

TEACHER IN ROLE WHOLE GROUP IN ROLE

Sit the group around you. Count the number of students. Go straight into the drama with the minimum of introduction. Some groups will cope with the following being your first words, if you have made a contract with them previously.

> Good morning class of 2017. Well, here we all are, the last week has finally arrived. Who'd have thought seven years ago that only you would have made it? Sitting in front of me are the finest trainee astronauts in the world today, left out of 350 who started the course. As your tutor, I am very proud of you indeed, very proud. Seven years of hard training ends tomorrow, with the passing out ceremony, hosted by the leader of the United Nations. If you get it right tomorrow then you'll all qualify. It should be a piece of cake, but if you do get it wrong, she might not give you your badge! However, all you have to do is operate in 3/4/5's shuttle simulators, performing an emergency landing on an uninhabited planet. Use the rest of today to practise, then we'll show her tomorrow. Good luck!

That might be enough information, but some groups may need you to stop the play and clarify out of role that they are to:

SMALL GROUP IMPROVISATION

Split into 3/4/5 groups and do a presentation of their idea of what an emergency landing of a space shuttle might be like.

Give them about 15-20 minutes to practise this. As you go around, stress the importance of language – technical yet economical.

TEACHER IN ROLE AS TUTOR

> The Leader of the United Nations is now in the building, you have about five minutes to finish off and set up.

> OK, she's at the end of the corridor – places everyone. Remember to salute when she comes in, and get in a straight line across here when we've all finished.

(It is probably better if you can get someone else as a partner in role. If not, a simple item of costume can aid the student's belief).

TEACHER IN ROLE	Thank you everyone – please continue
PUPILS PRESENT THEIR LANDINGS	After they have all finished, the Leader of the United Nations delivers her speech. Remind them (using gesture) to get into a line.

Visiting every one of you today has been a rare privilege. Such fine, talented people, all prepared to do anything to serve your world. You really are a credit to your race. It now only remains for me to swear with you the oath of allegiance and to present you with your badges.

SWEAR THE OATH

Please raise your right hands and repeat after me .... I DO SOLEMNLY SWEAR ...... TO OBEY ALL ORDERS .... AT ALL TIMES .... WITHOUT QUESTION. Please lower your arms and give yourselves a big round of applause.

PRESENT BADGE

The leader then goes down the line, shakes hands with each of the astronauts and gives them their badge (stick onto shoulder or give to them to stick on). Each badge reads 'ASTRONAUT – CLASS 1'.

You are now fully qualified astronauts – Well done!

TEACHER IN ROLE

Usually at this point you all get a well deserved holiday, time to be with your families and have a huge party. However, this is not the case for you people. We have for you a mission of monumental importance. A new planet has been discovered in a far off solar system, one that we believe may be very similar to Earth. Your mission is to travel to this planet. Once there, you will open your orders to find out the precise details of the mission. At this stage, all details must remain top secret. The flight to the planet will last one year each way, so you will be cryogenically frozen. Are there any questions?

NARRATION

CLARIFICATION	Answer in role first, then out of role if necessary.
TEACHER IN ROLE	You leave tomorrow! I suggest tonight you get some sleep. You are allowed to make just one phone call.
TELEPHONE TALK	Go and find a space away from anyone else. Sit on the floor. You can only make one phone call. Decide who is the person you are going to ring. Ring them now, imagine their side of the conversation and speak out yours.

Is there anyone who would like to share their phone call with us? |
DISCUSSION	What would it be like to be away from your family for over two years? Were they very proud of you? How much did you tell them about the mission?
DEFINE SPACE BUILD SHIP	Let's build the space shuttle that we are going to travel on. What do we need? How can we build it? What shall we use? Where shall we put it? We'll need some space over to use as the planet once we have landed.
DEFINE ROLES	What jobs do we all do? Where is the navigator going to go? Where are the cryogenic sleeping compartments going to be? Are we going to have a captain.?

Once the ship is built, place the orders in a sealed envelope:

LOCATE AN ALIEN. BRING IT BACK TO EARTH, ALIVE.

NARRATION	Right, now the ship's finished could you all find a space and lie down, close your eyes.

After the phone call home, everyone retired to their own room. They all thought about the mission ahead. What would it be like? What were their orders going to be? |

None of them slept particularly well.

In the morning they awoke.

Could you all now mime individually to my instructions.

They dressed..... and had breakfast. Silently they reported to the departure lounge. Then they entered the shuttle.

Can you freeze please.

They all knew their jobs and the take-off procedure. Soon they would be away from Earth, the computer guiding them to the new planet, whilst they slept in the freezing chambers.

WHOLE GROUP
IN ROLE

Can we now let the play run until we are all frozen in the chambers.

Stay frozen and just listen for a moment.

NARRATION

The year's journey passed as if it were a second. The ship's computer guided them into orbit of the new planet. When the crew awoke, they would see an incredibly beautiful place, blue oceans, beautiful forests, magnificent mountains, a place that looked like the Garden of Eden.

Start to mime now.

On the second orbit, each crew member slowly and stiffly started to awake. Gradually they made their way to the viewing gallery and watched the beautiful sight beneath them. Imagine the beauty of the planet as you listen to this music.

(Play whatever music is appropriate to suggest awe and wonder).

NARRATION

Just listen to me again please.

The crew snapped themselves out of the spell and set about their tasks. They had to land the ship, secure it, open their orders, and begin their exploration of the planet. Let's run the play.

They open the orders. As above:- LOCATE AN ALIEN, BRING IT BACK TO EARTH, ALIVE.

WHOLE GROUP IN ROLE

Here they can explore, usually they split into smaller groups naturally. You may wish to intervene and structure their activities or tasks, establishing roles such as archaeologists, food scientists, geologists etc. Manipulate away from options of weapons experts and trainers etc.

TEACHER IN ROLE

Teacher in role enters as the alien. No costume, but smile and appear helpless, no threat at all. It works best if you appear only to one group, a group who you think will support you (by support I mean not 'blow you away' immediately).

Hello, what are you doing on my planet? There's only a few of us left, soon there will only be two, that's what the book tells us. Our planet used to have machines, we believe they are wrong, they caused the Great War, the planet was bad and nearly destroyed. Now it is beautiful again. When there are only two of us left, we will start the new race of people. They call me Adam.

You get the idea. The dilemma is, do they obey their orders, they have sworn to do so, or do they save the Adam character and the race of people that will result?

WHOLE GROUP IN ROLE

From here you just have to let the play run.

Branch Planning

Useful things you can build in:

- Establish a radio link to Earth, put pressure on them to decide what to do.

- Small group improvisation: what would happen to Adam when he got back to Earth?

- Small group improvisation: What their families would do if they found out that their son or daughter had broken their oath.

Space Mission

Step	Reason	Convention	Emphasis
1 Teacher in role as trainer. Group in role as astronauts	Establishes belief	Teacher in role/whole group in role	Length of training. Need to pass tomorrow
2 Small groups	To have a performance for Leader of UN to judge	Small group improvisation	Importance of language
3 Teacher in role. Group in role	Establishes role as astronauts	Teacher in role	Establish role with seriousness
4 Performing work	Begins to establish their success	Presentations	Take very seriously
5 Group in role as astronauts. Teacher in role as Leader of UN	Creates self pride	Present badges	Use touch
6 Teacher in role as Leader of UN	Platform for the dilemma later on	Swear the oath	Seriousness of approach crucial
7 Teacher in role as Leader of UN	Provides information	Teacher in role/ narration	Stress open orders
8 Individual work	Reinforces the fact they are leaving	Exercise	Make sure they work on their own
9 Creating new imaginary space	Creates new working areas	Define the space	Leave room for the planet
10 Discussion/choosing	Preparing for work on the planet	Define roles	Variety of abilities
11 Miming to narration	Speeds up the drama	Mime/movement to narration	Music is very important
12 Astronauts exploring	Need to feel the freedom of their role	Whole group in role	Let them go!
13 Group as astronauts – teacher as alien	Injects the dilemma	Teacher in role or Pupils in role	Go to a group who will be supportive of you

To Be Or Not To Be

Used with Upper Primary, Secondary, 16+, Undergraduates, PGCE, In-Service and community groups.

Aim

to develop an understanding of the concept of ethical decision making.

Learning Outcomes

Drama Skills/Knowledge	Social Skills	Possible Learning Areas
Adopt a role	Be sensitive to the views of others	Ethical decisions
Use mime & gesture appropriately		Values & beliefs (personal)
Empathise with an imaginary character	Defend an adopted viewpoint	Values & beliefs (of other cultures)
William Shakespeare	Respect others' points of view	Forgiveness & mercy
Hamlet		Revenge
	Empathise with the difficult decisions people have to make in life	

Resources

Two cloaks – one black if possible, one sword, one copy of *Hamlet*, tape player, tape containing *To be or not to be* soliloquy (or this can be read by a member of the group) or a printed copy of the text (p89), large paper and pens, tape with some appropriate period music.

DEFINE SPACE

Alter space from its usual appearance. Place the chairs in a circle with a chair positioned just outside it. Place the black cloak in the centre of the circle with the sword and a copy of *Hamlet* arranged on it.

CONTRACT

Our work this session starts with a consideration of quite a difficult concept, that of 'ethical decisions'. This might mean nothing to you at the moment but by the end of the first session, you should have a good grasp of what it can mean. The work is initially based on Shakespeare's *Hamlet*. You do not need to know anything about the play. If you do, all well and good. Again, by the end of the session you will have explored and come to know part of Shakespeare's play.

(Put the sword, cloak and text outside the circle on the separate chair).

This should give us a good basis to develop the drama in directions that you then choose.

This first session will take the form of a game, work in pairs, smaller groups, whole group, individual response, small group with discussion in-between. At the end of the session, I want us to decide which way we could develop the drama over the next six weeks. Any questions?

GAMES

We are going to play a game which starts off with me giving each of you one of these words.

Write each of these on a separate sheet of paper and hold it up so the group can read it as you introduce it.

Reason, passion, tradition, religion.

Again at this moment they might not mean a great deal to you but they will become clearer. These are the elements of an 'ethical decision'.

Write this down on a separate sheet and let everyone see it.

Remember which word you are given as I come round and point at you. Reason, passion, tradition, religion, reason, passion, tradition....etc.

Right round the circle. Then remove the chair you have been sitting on.

All the reasons put your hands up, all the passions, all the traditions etc. Now put them down. This time, if I say one of these words as I stand in the middle of the circle, all the people with that word change places. As there is one chair short, someone will always end up in the middle. Let's try it slowly.

e.g. call out 'reason'.

Has everyone got the hang of it? Each time you end up in the middle, you call out one of the four words.

Play the game until every word has had a couple of turns.

Let us introduce another word, or rather phrase, 'ethical decision'. Now you have a fifth choice. If you say this, then everyone has to change place.

Play the game until everyone feels comfortable with the words.

As well as playing a game, you will have learnt what are the main elements involved in making an ethical decision. For the time being, we will put them on one side but come back to them later in our drama.

DEFINE THE SPACE	For our drama to happen we need to agree on the space we are working in. We need a court. In *Hamlet* it is called Elsinore.......

Write it out.

..... which was in Denmark. If this was to be the King's courtroom where would the throne be? How would these chairs be set out? If the King was to enter where would he enter from?

PREPARED ROLE RE-ENACTMENT	Would someone take on the role of the King and just walk in so that we can see what it looks like? This role does a lot of watching and thinking but not a lot of talking. Here is a cloak for you.

A piece of material if no cloak is available.

Let's just try you walking in. What sort of bow should we do as he enters? When do we stop doing it? Okay let's try it.

Re-enactment takes place.

Well done, we have the King. Could you just sit a little back from the circle and I will come and talk to you in a while.

TEACHER IN ROLE	I will take on the role of Prince Hamlet when I wear this cloak and carry this sword. So we have the King and the Prince – that leaves everyone else.

COLLECTIVE ROLE MIME	To start the drama I would like you to become travelling players. In the times when Shakespeare was writing and before, in medieval times, there were entertainers who travelled from court to court to perform for royalty. In

Shakespeare's play *Hamlet* there is just such a group and they have a very important role within the play.

I wonder what sort of entertainers and performers there might have been?

Take suggestions.

Will each of you, without telling even the person next to you, decide if you had a chance to be a player in those times, (the play was written in 1600-1, by the way) what would you be?

Give time for thought.

Rather than tell us outright, I would like you to quickly mime what you do and we will guess even more quickly what it is. What, for example would I be?

Mime a juggler, a singer etc.

Do not worry if someone does what you have thought of. There was bound to have been more than one singer, dancer, fire eater.

Go round the circle and keep it pacey to save any embarrassment. To individuals who you think can take it, talk to them in role e.g. 'Tell me, no one is listening, have you ever hurt yourself blowing fire?'

ROLE WORK
IN PAIRS

We now have our roles and we know where the action is going to take place. Before we start the action which commences in our drama with you entering the court, I just want to go quickly into the past. This could be helpful later. Get into pairs.

You have visited the court every year for years. You have seen this small boy grow up into a young man and have grown very fond of him. He loves your performances and spends every moment he can in your company when you visit Elsinore.

Think for a minute of an anecdote or past memory of Hamlet as a young boy or teenager.

Model this by turning to the person next to you.

'He always ran up to show me his juggling. One day, when he was about seven he threw a ball up and it never came down. It landed on a ledge in the courtroom. Well he laughed and laughed and laughed'.

Tell your anecdotes to your partner and then swap. Okay, think for a minute. The next time you speak it will be in role to your partner.

Make sure the reminiscences are positive ones built on your modelled examples. The response is being clearly manipulated here to produce a generally lively, mischievous, fun loving child. Let the paired reminiscences carry on until everyone seems to have had a say but before everything is quiet. Whilst this is going on, go across to the 'King'.

Listen carefully and watch everything that Hamlet does as it is going to seriously affect you. Your role in the drama is important. You are not in fact Hamlet's father, you are his uncle. To get on the throne you have killed your own brother, Hamlet's father. What is more, you have married the former King's wife. You strongly suspect that Hamlet knows about this but are not sure. In a while all the players will, under Hamlet's direction, present a play for you. This play mirrors your killing of the king. When they perform it, they will all be watching you. Think how you can show a mounting guilt just by your body language as you watch the play. At a point when the tension is high and you feel it reaches a dramatic climax, stand up and run out of the court. Sit down beyond the circle and listen in to what happens next. Any questions?

This can be done verbally or with the above details on a card that the individual reads and then asks you any questions he or she needs to know. Pull the group together.

DISCUSSION

Would you share some of your reminiscences with us?

Select a pair that have been working well.

Any one else?

Listen to as many anecdotes and memories as is reasonable.

ROLE ON THE WALL

Draw a role on the wall figure that looks quite small.

Let's choose an age for this young Hamlet we have been reminiscing about. How old do you think?

Select or compromise on suggestions; e.g. seven years old.

From the reminiscences we have just heard, give me some adjectives, some words to describe the character of young Hamlet.

Write down each word as it is given around the figure. Ask supplementary questions if possible e.g. if one of the group says 'sense of humour' press for examples. If someone says something that does not hold true with the reminiscences, ask the group if they know another word which could perhaps capture this feeling, but which would be acceptable to all. Read out all the words when no more are offered.

Take another piece of paper and draw a bigger role on the wall.

We are coming up to the very start of the play and our drama now. Many years have passed. How old should we say he is now as a young man?

Agree an age.

You have visited the court every year for years and have always, even last year, seen the young Hamlet who was always the ......

Read out the positive adjectives on the first role on the wall...

But this year, when you turn up expecting to see just that, you see that Hamlet has changed greatly. Watch him now. The last time you saw him was when you visited last year, he looked well and happy. What do you see now?

Pick up the visual signals which could give an insight into this e.g. watch and be prepared to say what you see and exactly what actions suggest what feelings and emotions.

You have all mimed earlier. I will do one now. When I finish I will ask you for adjectives that describe Hamlet at the start of our drama and in Act 3 Scene 1 of Shakespeare's play. Whilst I am doing this mime, I will put on a tape/ask someone to read one of the most famous passages in *Hamlet*. It is the *To be or not to be* speech. You can watch and/or listen for clues. I am also going to ask the King to come into the circle and sit on his throne. Don't join in King, but it would help me if I could use you in this mime.

TEACHER IN ROLE

The speech starts or is read.

As teacher in role here the emphasis is on showing the anger, sorrow, sadness, confidence, uncertainty and confusion in Hamlet's mind. Actions with the sword suggest at various points options such as killing the King, killing himself, leaving the whole thing behind him, hurting himself with the blade, perhaps pulling it through his clenched hand.

ROLE ON THE WALL

What did you see or hear?

Write down all the responses. Compare this with the other role on the wall and then put them side by side.

Thanks for all those words. Let us now find out what has bought him to this and caused such a change.

WHOLE
GROUP
ROLE PLAY

We are now at the point when Hamlet meets the travelling players. We are in the courtyard when the action starts. The travelling players have just arrived. How long have they been travelling for since their last court performance in another country? What time should they arrive? How do you think they are feeling when they start to unpack their wagons and perhaps get things ready and rehearse for the performance that night? I'll let the action run for a few minutes and then enter as Hamlet. I guess when they see him they will be shocked or surprised by the change in him and would gather round. Any questions?

Run the role play. Hamlet is friendly, but riddled with the need to know beyond reasonable doubt that his own uncle did in fact kill his father and if his own mother was party to this. The company are given access to this. Teacher in role can feed lines from the play into this to make them accessible. He reluctantly tells the players of his fears and the story of the death. He then asks them to act it for him in the form of *The Murder of Gonzago* (A simplified version of the play within the play in *Hamlet*). *The play's the thing wherein we'll catch the conscience of the King.*

Teacher lets the class mime through the 'murder' and helps fill in detail, quickly finding roles for all the class e.g. King / Queen / uncle / uncle's deafmutes (look-outs) / the orchard and arbour (individuals can become statues and part of the orchard) / guests at the wedding feast / etc.

Focus on catching the conscience of the King, a game element. This re-enactment should be fun. The group should be surprised that they have so quickly put this mime show together.

As you recall, the scene takes place in the royal gardens. The setting was fascinatingly created by all of you representing statues, urns, shrubs and trees.

Motion to the group to take up these positions.

Into the garden step a king and queen .....do we have someone willing to take on these roles?......Very much in love with each other they hold hands. He then lies down to sleep upon the grass and she blows him a kiss and leaves. No sooner has she left than the wicked brother of the sleeping king enters accompanied by a group of deaf mutes.

Motion to others to take on these roles.

When they nod that the coast is clear, he takes from his pocket a small phial of poison and lets a drop fall into the king's ear. The king now falls silently from deep sleep into death. His wicked brother signals to the mutes and they leave. Re-enter the queen who thinks her husband is still sleeping. She tenderly touches him to find he is dead. She protests her grief and turns to run from the garden but runs instead straight into the arms of the murderer. He asks what is the matter, then sees the body. He protests his grief as do the mutes who have accompanied him. Members of the court attend the funeral

Motion others to take on these roles.

Grave diggers bury the body.

Motion to others to take on these roles.

A blessing is given by the priest.

Motion to someone else to take on this role.

TEACHER IN ROLE **WHOLE GROUP** **ROLE PLAY** **PERFORMANCE** **PREPARED ROLE**	Food is served

Motion to anyone who is left to take on these roles.

> And here is the most terrible part of all...the food used at the funeral serves also for the wedding feast of the queen and the wicked brother who is now crowned king. This is the play that the King must see. Thank you. In your places – the King approaches.

Motion for the King to approach and everyone else to re-enact the entrance of the King rehearsed at the beginning of the session. Put on music as a loud backdrop to this piece. As Hamlet, walk behind the players and keep urging them to watch the King for signs of conscience and guilt.

BRIEF PREPARED ROLE

As they get ready to run through, quickly remind the King to flee from the room at the point when he or she feels the tension is greatest.

RE-ENACTMENT OF PERFORMANCE & ROLEPLAY

Re-enactment with tape music playing (period music or as appropriate to give more atmosphere to this performance).

As the King flees, the music is stopped dead. As Hamlet, approach the players.

> He is guilty – did you see it?

Get them to tell you if they saw physical signs of his guilt. At the appropriate moment switch to narrative.

NARRATION

> And so the players left the court and Hamlet bade farewell to his friends whose carts he had already had treasure put upon so they could flee quickly. Hamlet, full of resolution, ran to the King's room and was just about to kick open the door, when all the indecision and doubt that had beset him before fell upon him once again.

REFLECTION ON ACTION	Bring the group back into a circle. Out of role, outline some of the main options Hamlet has open to him e.g. kill the King / kill himself / try to carry on living. What else could he do?
MIND PARTS	Remind the group about reason / passion / tradition / religion and how these were elements in making an ethical decision. Give an explanation of each element briefly and place each word which you wrote earlier in the drama at a different point of the circle e.g.

> Passion would probably say 'Kill him, Kill him!' What by contrast might Reason say? What would Religion say if Hamlet was a Christian? What would it say if he was a Buddhist? What is the Tradition of the land Elsinore is in? Is it revenge or do courts decide? etc.

It is essential that the group have a grasp of these key words but they will need to be reassured that their understanding of these will develop as the drama progresses. An element of trust has to be asked for here. It is through doing the drama that we may come to understand these terms more fully.

Ask the group to choose which part of Hamlet's mind they would like to become and then to go and sit by the word in that part of the circle.

TEACHER IN ROLE MIND PARTS	When he listens to that part of his mind that is you, you will have to deal with him in the mood you find him in. Try to deal with the decision he appears to have made at that moment, always being aware that this could suddenly swing again. You can only try to persuade him when his sword is touching your piece of paper.

Have a practice, probably with 'passion' and emphasise the 'broken record technique' i.e. they can keep on saying the same thing over and over again but as soon as the sword lifts off, they must stop even in mid-sentence. Try this and emphasise the game element to this, i.e. who is going to influence Hamlet the most.

Keep turning from one mind part to the other and really build interaction up. Ask supplementary questions, get angry with some parts of your mind, side with others, keep switching, monitor the pace.

Have key questions ready, e.g. If the 'Religion' group says:

'Thou shalt not kill' agree with them but then suddenly throw back:

But the bible says 'An eye for an eye, a tooth for a tooth.'

e.g. If the Reason group says:

'Think carefully about the implications of killing him,' then throw back:

Logically I should kill him before he kills me.

After much listening and questioning, reach the point where you are about to make the decision. Atmosphere should have built by now and the level of engagement should be high.

| CONSCIENCE ALLEY |

Ask the group to form into two lines. Each person now has the chance to try to persuade you for the last time. Ask the class to decide what they are going to say as you pass by. There is a chance to change your 'mindpart' now. Let them know that you, in role as Hamlet, are going to listen to the strength and quality of the arguments given and make your decision according to what you hear. This will decide the end of this version of Hamlet. At the end of this long line stands the King.

| TEACHER IN ROLE MODELS POSSIBLE ACTION |

Hamlet has a sword in his hand. Recap his options. Kill the King, kill himself, walk away etc. Rehearse in front of the class a practical action that will signify a particular decision which must be made by the time you reach a copy of *Hamlet* placed on the floor, just in front of the King, e.g. kill the King by thrusting the sword under the King's arm, the King's head falls on his chest, freeze. The person playing the King quickly rehearses this moment (this saves laughter later which may be inappropriate if this form of action is taken). The others are similarly rehearsed using the group's suggestions. The emphasis is on letting the group know that Hamlet's ethical decision is now in their hands. Run the action by walking very slowly down the corridor. At the final moment make your decision according to the quality and strength of argument heard in the walk down conscience alley.

DISCUSSION

Bring the group back into a circle and tell them what led you to make that particular decision. Reflect on learning outcomes and see in which direction the group want to go now.

Branch Planning

All of these options could be followed in a longer project or one could be explored in detail, or the group may suggest other possibilities.

Use the pretext as a way of accessing the text e.g. you could return to the *To be or not to be* speech and experiment with verse speaking. You could re-enact the final scene in the last act and explore how Shakespeare handled this. You could look at how Ophelia is caught up in Hamlet's world and perhaps dies because of it. You could explore specific lines from the text which open up further areas for drama such as predestination and fate. For example Hamlet's lines:
'There's a divinity that shapes our ends,
Rough-hew them how we will.' (Act V Sc.II)

At the simplest level you could ask the group to find out how Shakespeare finished his play. The motivation will be there. Alternatively you could ask the group to reflect individually on the way they personally make decisions e.g.

Are you the sort of person who is ruled by passion? Do you make decisions on feelings? Are you more the reasoning type? Would you like to listen to 'passion' more? Does religion play a part in the way you make decisions? What family traditions have influenced you? Think of the phrases that were said to you again and again in your youth or are said to you every week at home.

Now think of a personal ethical decision that you have
made in the past, are facing now, or may in the future.
Split into friendship groups and those who wish to share
these, do so.

These could then be shared with the agreement of the participants and
form the basis for the coming weeks' drama work.

Ask the group to think about ethical decisions people have to make in
society. Can they think of examples? These could be at local, national or
international levels.

For example: local – vandalism; national – closing down a naval dockyard, a
coal mine; international – the occupation of territories of one country by
another. The ethical dimension of one or some of the group's suggestions
could be explored through a drama or piece of theatre.

Hamlet – Act 3, Scene 1

To be, or not to be: that is the question:
Whether 'tis nobler in the mind to suffer
The slings and arrows of outrageous fortune,
Or to take arms against a sea of troubles,
And by opposing end them? To die: to sleep;
No more; and by a sleep to say we end
The heart-ache and the thousand natural shocks
That flesh is heir to, 'tis a consummation
Devoutly to be wish'd. To die, to sleep;
To sleep: perchance to dream: ay, there's the rub;
For in that sleep of death what dreams may come
When we have shuffled off this mortal coil,
Must give us pause: there's the respect
That makes calamity of so long life;
For who would bear the whips and scorns of time,
The oppressor's wrong, the proud man's contumely,
The pangs of despised love, the law's delay,
The insolence of office and the spurns
That patient merit of the unworthy takes,
When he himself might his quietus make
With a bare bodkin? who would fardels bear,
To grunt and sweat under a weary life,
But that the dread of something after death,
The undiscover'd country from whose bourn
No traveller returns, puzzles the will,
And makes us rather bear those ills we have
Than fly to others we know not of?
Thus conscience does make cowards of us all;
And thus the native hue of resolution
Is sicklied o'er with the pale cast of thought,
And enterprises of great pitch and moment
With this regard their currents turn awry,
And lose the name of action.

To Be or Not To Be

Step	Reason	Convention	Emphasis
1 Arrange the chairs in a circle with one chair outside it. Place a black cloak in the centre with a copy of 'Hamlet' on it, and a sword next to that	Engages interest and encourages speculation	Define space	The sword should be a 'safety foil' if possible. The safety element needs stressing before the group enters
2 We will be looking at the concept of ethical decision making and 'Hamlet'	Clarifies the focus of the work	Contract	You do not need to know anything about ethical decisions or 'Hamlet'. As usual your ideas will be used to develop the drama over the next weeks
3 Let us play a game with four words which will be important in our drama. Move round the circle and point at each person in turn asking them to remember either 'Reason' 'Passion' 'Tradition' 'Religion'. Remove one chair from the circle. Call out one of the words. Swap places if it is your word. The person in the middle can then call another word. If you call 'Ethical Decision' you all move	The constituent parts of an 'ethical decision' are reason, passion, tradition and religion. Playing a game lodges them in the mind of the class to return to later in the drama	Game	Ask all the 'reasons' then, 'passions', etc. to raise their hands before playing in case anyone had misheard you. Play, yourself
4 How should we set the courtroom out?	Gives some ownership and control to the group	Define space	Use their ideas, combine them if necessary
5 Will someone play the King? Practise the King's entrance	This can be used later in the drama	Prepared role re-enactment	The King is all-powerful. It is a quiet, observant role initially
6 Teacher takes on role of Hamlet symbolised by the sword and cloak	To be able to challenge from within the drama as it progresses	Teacher in role	In the coming weeks, some of you or all of you will take on this role

Step	Reason	Convention	Emphasis
7 The rest of the group are to be travelling players. What would you be, given a choice as a player e.g. juggler. A minute to think then we will go round the circle and guess as you mime	To begin to build roles made from personal choice	Collective role Mime	Keep the guessing of mimes quick to avoid embarrassment
8 Let us go back in time to when Hamlet was a young boy. How old? He used to love the travelling players and got up to all sorts of mischief when they visited the castle. Begin reminiscing about the tricks he got up to with you all those years ago. Do this in pairs	This begins to establish the perspective of the players	Role work in pairs	Give an example 'Do you remember when he cut my tightrope in half?' Keep the anecdotes flowing. You only have a few minutes
9 Whilst the pair work is in progress, let the volunteer playing the King know that Hamlet suspects him of killing his father and is very upset as he has married his mother. In a while the players will show a play revealing this. Think how through body language, this guilt can be shown. Before the end of the play leave the room	To prepare the role and give the volunteer a challenge in drama terms of finding appropriate body language and responding to tension in having to choose the 'right' moment to flee	Prepared role	Make sure this volunteer is clear about the role and context knowing that they do not have to worry about instigating action at all
10 Share reminiscences	Builds context	Discussion	Join in with reminiscences and say you remember also. Ask questions to support anecdotes

Step	Reason	Convention	Emphasis
11 Draw a role of young Hamlet on the wall. Ask for adjectives to describe him. Move forward in time. Hamlet is now older. Draw another role on the wall and ask the group to watch you in role as Hamlet. When you finish, ask for words that describe Hamlet now	Focuses on Hamlet's character and dilemma	Role on the wall	Upgrade all suggestions. If instead of offering adjectives, reasons for the change are given, remind the group you only want words at this point but that their ideas will come in useful later
12 Group watches as teacher mimes the uncertainty in Hamlet's mind. Actions with the sword suggest various feelings. Get someone to read the 'To be or not to be' speech	Gives the group a chance to read action. Introduces the big change there has been in his character	Teacher in role Mime Soundtrack	Ask the group to 'read' your actions. Use the King as a focus. This can inject much tension. They can watch and/or listen to the words
13 Write down adjectives	Focuses observations and tests understanding	Role on the wall	Focus on the words that describe action not the reasons for it
14 The players arrive. Hamlet asks them to perform a play to 'catch the conscience of the King'. He rehearses the murder of Gonzago.	Allows the group to be successful very quickly in mounting a performance	Whole group role play Teacher in role	Stress the friendship, trust and loyalty between you and the players in role
15 Run the play for the King. In role, encourage the group to watch the King. Put on music as a backdrop for the play	Adds another layer of tension to the drama and high level of performance success	Teacher in role Whole group role play Prepared role Performance	Urge everyone to 'read' the King for signs of guilt
16 Remind the King to flee when he feels tension is right	Gives the volunteer playing the King a chance to clarify action	Prepared role	Ask the King not to leave the room totally, as he needs to listen in.

Step	Reason	Convention	Emphasis
17 Re-enact the play. Stop the music when the King flees	Adds tension	Re-enactment of performance and role play	Ask did they see guilt?
18 Drop into narrative commentary. 'Hamlet said farewell to the players and went to kill the King. Just before he got to his room all the indecision fell upon him again'	Focuses the dramatic action	Narrative	Do not let the players feel uncomfortable. Narrate them away from the action
19 Bring the group back into a circle. What can Hamlet do now? What are the options?	Reintroduces ethical decision making	Reflection on action	Clarify the concrete options he now has
20 Ask the group to choose either Reason, Passion, Tradition or Religion and to argue these within Hamlet's mind	Begins to illuminate what the constituent parts of an ethical decision are	Mind parts	Ask the group if they remember the words they played the game with earlier in the drama
21 Stand in the middle of the four groups. When you point your sword at a group, they must convince you from the perspective of their chosen word, what to do	Deepens commitment	Teacher in role Mind parts	Stress the arguments can be repeated. The aim is to convince
22 Each person now has a chance to influence and decide what decision Hamlet makes in this play	Allows individuals to reflect upon their attitude to revenge	Conscience alley /corridor	These do not have to be your personal beliefs and attitudes
23 Agree upon symbolic actions that represent the various options for Hamlet	To keep the emphasis on the decision not on the melodramatics of the situation	Teacher in role models possible action	Keep the options clear and distinct. The narrative after the decision cannot be prejudged
24 'What happened in Shakespeare's play?' 'What ethical decisions have you made in your lives?'	To focus either on text or personal and social development	Discussion	Explain why you made the particular decision you did

Gangs

Used with Upper Primary, Secondary, 16+, Undergraduates, PGCE & In-Service

Aim

to provide, through the dramatic focus, parallels with the group's own current or previous circumstances, which could be explored if they are willing.

Learning Outcomes

Drama Skills/Knowledge	Social Skills	Possible Learning Areas
Be responsible for sustaining and developing a number of contrasting roles	Speaking and listening skills	Peer group pressure
	Fostering a sense of group identity	Adolescence
Model appropriate language register, vocabulary and tone within the drama		Teenage culture
	Express emotions and feelings in a constructive way	
Experiment with a number of drama conventions		

Resources

Paper, sticky labels, felts, tape player, music chosen by the class in groups.

GAMES	Split the group into two using the numbers game;

Walk – when I shout out a number, get into groups of that size.

Try this with 2,4,5,6 or whatever. End on 15 or what is half of the group.

Play tee-ak-ee-allio.

The players divide into two teams. Each team has a base in a corner of the room. The object of the game is to capture the opposing players by tapping them on the head and calling 'tee-ak'. Once touched, the captive goes to the enemy base and can only be released from this by one of his own side running through the base shouting 'tee-ak-ee-allio'. He can then rejoin the game, which continues until one side manages to capture all the opposing players at one time – as described by Clive Barker (Barker, C. 1980, *Theatre Games*, Methuen).

We find it more successful to place ribbon over a player's wrist, they are caught if this falls to the floor or is captured by an opponent.

COMPLETION OF TASKS	Now the group is in two halves that feel competitive towards each other. Set them the following tasks:

You are going to be a gang.

1. Decide where your gang base is and build it.

2. Give your gang a name and design a badge for it.

3. Decide how your gang is to be governed, for instance will you have a leader?

4. Decide on a uniform – could you all wear the same for next week's session?

5. For next session decide on a piece of music that is to be your gang's theme.

It is helpful if there is a gap of time here. Time to go away and do some research is valuable for the quality of the ensuing drama.

HALF GROUP IMROVISATION	Using your gang base as the setting, show us what everyday life is like in your gang. Try to bring out the structure of how the gang is run.

Show and discuss.

MOVEMENT PIECE	At some point in this drama there is going to be a gang fight. The conflict will be displayed by showing each other movement pieces, to the music you have chosen. The best piece of movement will be the top gang. You've got the rest of this session to sort it out.

Give them enough time to practise, then share the dances.

Sit the group in a circle. Go straight into the drama.

WHOLE GROUP IN ROLE – A MEETING	Thank you all for coming today at such short notice. I am Tom Smith, Head of the Juvenile Crime Prevention Unit. As we all know, juvenile crime in this area has become a real problem – caused largely by these gangs. We're all here today to try and sort out a way forward. Perhaps we could introduce ourselves and state our interest.

Individuals may take on the role of police, social workers, parents, council officials etc. If it does not flow, then it may be necessary to stop the drama and discuss roles and points of view.

At the meeting, steer the decision towards giving the youths something to do. (The group often comes up with this but the drama may go off on a totally different track).

SMALL GROUP PLANNING

Make a sum of money available, say £500,000.

Move individuals into small groups. The task is to design a facility that would be ideal for teenagers and would prevent them getting into trouble. This can continue for several sessions if each is then presented.

EVALUATION

Discuss/evaluate the work with the pupils.

> Why is there nothing like this in our area? If there is, does it work? Why do people join gangs? What is it like being a teenager?

Branch Planning

Use the work as a way into *Romeo and Juliet*. What would happen if a person from one gang fell in love with a person from the other. Move from improvisation to text.

Gangs

Step		Reason	Convention	Emphasis
1	Game playing	Warm up Competitiveness Teams	Game	Keep physicality to a minimum. Sin-bin for rough play
2	Group planning	Establishes gang	Tasks out of role	Encourage competition
3	Group improvising	Deepens role	Improvisation	Stress ordinary, everyday life
4	Group dancing	Positive outlet for competitiveness	Movement	Feed in shapes, idea of story- telling through movement
5	Everyone in role	Reflection within the drama	Whole group in role	Establish a role for everyone
6	Planning/designing	To find a positive solution	Designing	What would they like in their area?

Developing a drama pretext – a planning example

Our planning tends to fall into 10 stages.

1. Identify an idea, issue, feeling, thought, image, concept, story text or theme.
2. Brainstorm content, images and conventions that possibly match ideas.
3. Identify possible learning outcomes that could be built in.
4. Re-work images and conventions in the light of possible learning outcomes.
5. First draft with tentative running order and backfill.
6. Second draft in preferred layout.
7. Identify resources that would enrich the learning.
8. Branch plan possible developments.
9. Clarify aims and learning outcomes.
10. Use with a group and refine in the light of experience.

Example – 'The Rains'

1. Identify an idea, issue, feeling, thought, image, concept, story, text or theme

(by yourself, or with the group, by brainstorming all ideas.)

A story is identified, in this example *The Rains*. It is based on an African (Ghanaian) story told originally to us by Inno Sorcy:

There is a time of year in the rainforests when the air goes yellow under a black sky and all the animals know the rainy season is about to begin. It starts with just one small drop on a single leaf but before long everything is washed flat by the force of the rain. Any animal who has not prepared shelter and gathered food before the rain starts, stands no chance of survival. Nothing can grow or survive in the months that make the rainy season.

On one such day, just as the heavens began to open up, a small squirrel sat in the entrance to his home at the top of a bank in a huge tree. He was feeling very pleased with himself because he was all prepared, and there is no cosier feeling than knowing you have got a dry home and enough food to see you through a difficult part of the year. His home was just the right size and very well protected. He had worked hard scraping out a small section of rotten wood in that huge tree. At first he did not know if he would be able to dig out a space big enough for himself. Luckily he had made enough room for a small bed under which he could store his precious food. **He tried hard for a full week to make it just a little bigger, but it was no use. Even a team of beavers could make no impression on the rest of the tree trunk which was as tough as steel. At least he knew there could only ever be one home in that tree and it was his.**

As he sat in the doorway, he saw the trickle of water running along the path at the bottom of the bank turn into a stream, then a river and then a raging torrent. Everything that was not secure in the forest was being washed away. A great log was sailing past when he saw something else flapping and struggling in the water trying hopelessly to fight against the current. 'Over here' he shouted and sure enough, even with the noise of the beating rain, the thing seemed to hear. It struggled to the bank and hung on to a root of his tree. It tried to climb the bank but it was so muddy that the thing slipped down to the water's edge and was nearly washed away. But it clung to the root and tried again, got further up, then slipped down, tried a third time and just made it to the top of the bank where it shook itself. As it did so, leaves, mud and bits of twigs were flung off and little Squirrel saw that it was a huge porcupine.

'Come inside and dry off,' said little Squirrel and Porcupine squeezed his way into the small, dry home. 'Have something to eat, please,' said little Squirrel. 'Lie on my bed, you must be exhausted'. Porcupine said nothing, only grunted, as he gobbled down the food and fell fast asleep. Soon, in spite of the noise of the rain, he was snoring away and little Squirrel realised that he too was very tired. It had been a long day.

Squirrel's house was really quite small, with room really only for one. Now Porcupine was on the bed there was only the floor space next to it to sleep on. He curled up in it and was just about drifting off to sleep when ping! – one of Porcupine's quills stuck in his side. 'Ow!' he shouted. Then – ping! – another struck as Porcupine turned over in his sleep again. 'Ouch!' he cried and 'Ouch!' again and this went on all night. Every time Porcupine turned over, Squirrel got pinged! Little Squirrel did not get a wink of sleep.

Porcupine woke up late the next morning. 'Good morning, Porcupine,' said Squirrel, 'I trust you feel well after eating so much and sleeping so well?' He got no reply and so carried on talking. **'As is the custom of our country, you are welcome to stay three nights and three days. What is mine is yours!'** Porcupine grunted again and said he was hungry. Squirrel gave him some more food and then some more. Porcupine spent the day eating and sleeping. He must be exhausted, thought Squirrel, what troubles he has been through. As he sat in the doorway watching the rain come down he could not help thinking of his precious food supply under the bed, getting lower and lower.

On the second night, Porcupine slept all night. Once again, every time he turned over – ping! – poor Squirrel on the floor got spiked. As he looked up at this huge creature in his bed, he thought he would not be able to make it through the night. It was just too much, but he knew the customs of his country. Only one more night to go, he said to himself.

Squirrel felt awful the next day. He tried, but he could not be civil to Porcupine. But he passed him food again and again. When his guest slept, he sat in his doorway and watched the water racing past.

On the third night, just as Porcupine was about to roll over and go to sleep, Squirrel could be patient no longer. He had worked hard to carve out his little home and stock it with food. This was steadily being eaten away, right in front of his own eyes. For two nights he had had no sleep. 'Porcupine! It is the custom of our country that you are my guest, for three days and three nights. You still are my guest, but I must sleep in my own bed tonight.' Porcupine muttered something, rolled off the bed and on to the floor and fell fast asleep.

Squirrel fell into his bed and was sinking into a deep sleep when – ping! – Porcupine moved on the floor and one of his quills went right through the mattress into Squirrel's side. 'Ouch!' he screamed, then ping! And ping again! All through the night.

The next morning, Squirrel was **so** angry. He had not slept a wink. He could not bring himself to speak a word. He could not even bear to give Porcupine food from under the bed but let him take it himself, which he quickly did. Finally, the light of the day began to give way to the night. It was the end of the third and final day.

Little Squirrel spoke at last. 'Porcupine, as is the custom of our country I have welcomed you as my guest for three days and three nights. What was mine has been yours. Now by the traditions of our country and all that is good, I wish you farewell and good luck. Good bye'.

Porcupine had now risen up and **filled the whole of the doorway. He looked down at little Squirrel and** looked him straight in the eyes for the first time since his arrival.

'What do you mean?' he grunted.

'I mean,' said Squirrel, 'That it is time for you to go. Goodbye!'

Porcupine spoke again: **'You mean that you are telling me to go out when night is about to fall, into the rain that will not stop for a month or more, into a land where all the food that has not been stored has been washed away, into a land where I have no shelter or chance of building one under the force of those torrential rains, a land that I may die in?'**

Squirrel said, 'I don't know about all that, but I am asking you to leave my home that I worked very hard to build and stock with food so that I would survive another year. Yes, I am telling you that you have got to go!'

'Squirrel, you do not mean this.'

'Porcupine! You just don't understand. You must leave. You don't see do you? You have a real problem!'

Porcupine settled himself firmly down in the doorway, looked straight into Squirrel's eyes again and said:

'I don't have a problem. You do!'

2. Brainstorm

content, images and conventions that suggest possibilities for matching ideas.

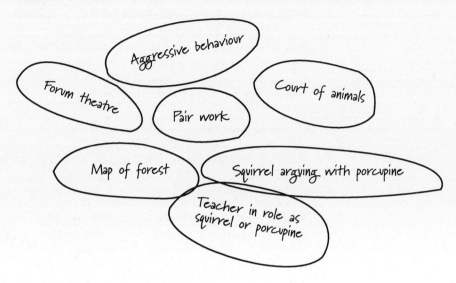

3. Identify possible learning outcomes

don't be too precious, just brainstorm them. This could be done under the headings of:

a. Drama and theatre skills and knowledge.

— role play, interacting in role

— voicework?

— manipulating plot

— allegory / analogy?   — role reversal?

b. Social and personal skills.

— presenting ideas

— relating the drama to their own life?

— role behaviour

c. Possible learning areas – lessons for life.

— assertiveness

— aggression / oppression

4. Roughly re-work images and conventions

in the light of the possible learning outcomes identified in step 3. Frames – roles, situation, focus and perspective should by now have begun to form. Put these into a spider diagram form.

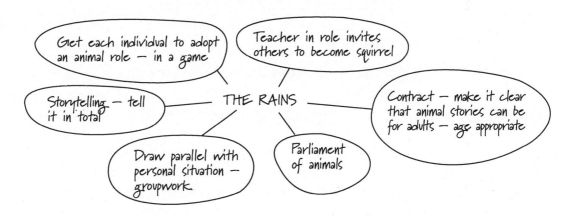

5. First draft

Try to create a tentative running order for these steps by listing them in the probable order the class would engage with them. Identify if there are any major breaks in the continuity of the steps. If there are gaps which would mean the class losing interest or understanding, try and backfill these. In other words, devise link steps that would be dramatically and theatrically engaging.

This is an important stage. Think of:

- hooking interest from the outset.

- do the steps build commitment and belief?

- are there clear tasks within the framework for the group to engage with and allow you as teacher to stand back?

- is each step clear in terms of roles, situation, focus and perspective?

---

1. Adopt an animal – rhyme it with your name, model this – Game.

2. Tell the story emphasising the defined space – Storytelling.

3. Try running a forum theatre session on solutions to this 'oppression' – Forum.

4. Use narration to manipulate action so the solution is difficult – Narration.

5. Try many 'solutions' – & involve all others in the role play – how?

6. Give all individuals a choice about whether he lives or dies if he is kicked out from the home.

7. Parable, analogy, allegory – Group work.

---

6. Second draft

Write out the pretext in your preferred form. Pay careful attention to structure and reasons for change in step, balance of conventions used, utilisation of drama elements, emphasis in terms of key pieces of information, phrases and questions to be asked. Put yourself in the position of the participants and literally imagine in specific detail what you would actually say and do in response to your own questions asked and tasks set.

Is there an underlying tension or game to the drama? Make amendments accordingly

1. Contract. Explain 'dilemma story' in 'African' (Ghanaian) tradition.

2. Game. Animals names to rhyme with own name.

3. Define space. Use a piece of material. African?

4. Storytelling. Emphasis on no more room and the impossibility of surviving in the rains with no home or food; i.e. constraints and facts. Emphasise these when telling the story (they are marked in bold type in our text).

5. Key question. What can Squirrel do?

6. Clarify this-recap. Allow for questions.

7. Teacher-in-role; group as audience. Let role drop for a moment.

8. Forum. Encourage many to try ideas. Keep it pacey.

9. The solution must be the start of a next phase — give two options.
   a) Porcupine dies   b) He lives, but is hurt
   Focus the group on the 'consequences of their actions'

10. Whole group role play. Teacher and group as rulers of forest. Watch Squirrel's action and take him before the parliament of animals.

7. Add a resource list

and identify steps that could be enriched or enhanced by theatrical resources such as lighting, music, props and set.

African (Ghanaian) material — or something suitable to represent the home of Squirrel.

8. Branch plan

in terms of identifying tasks or conventions not used in the main structure that could be used if the pretext finishes quickly or does not take off.

> Re-track Porcupine's past life – What has made him like that?
> Analogy & parallel situations (older groups)
> Sculpture work
> Song and movement (younger groups)
> Rain song?

9. Clarify your aims

- what the teacher intends and hopes to do.

Your learning outcomes

– what the students will be able to do.

Introduce the idea that drama can be about a battle of wits and intelligence as well as emotional exploration. The idea of the 'game of drama.'

Skills & Understanding	Social	Possible Learning
Select own material/ voice skills/ allegory	Role behaviour Present ideas	Oppression & Assertiveness

---

10. Use the pretext with a class

and see what works, what you have to add, lose or modify. Keep on modifying it into a 'seasoned pretext'.

The Rains

Based on a story from Ghana, Africa, told to us by Inno Sorcy.

Aims

To help the group begin to take pleasure in the 'game of drama'.
To provide a quality input that will launch a drama project.

Learning Outcomes

Drama skills/Knowledge	Social Skills	Possible Learning Areas
Select own material about dramatic potential	Make agreement	Assertiveness
Call upon a range of subtle skills in voice and movement	Role Behaviour	Oppression
	Relate knowledge to context	Personal ways of handling difficulties
		Fairness, justice and compassion
Develop appropriate drama forms	Plan and present ideas	Knowledge of African 'Ghanaian' culture, traditions
Understand and use the terms 'allegory', 'culture' and 'analogy'		
Develop an understanding of the 'game of drama'		

Resources

Piece of African material to represent Squirrel's home.

Sit the class in a circle.

CONTRACT

In this drama we are going to explore an 'African dilemma story'. In certain parts of Africa, such as Ghana, stories are told as a means of educating children in the family home. Some nights, after the evening meal, the family will gather and parents will tell a story which will finish at a point where there is a dilemma, a choice to be made, which is not easy for the character involved. The family discuss what each of them would do and a lot of learning gets done in the process. We are going to explore such a dilemma story.

This story is about animals but that does not mean it is for children. As in a lot of cultures, an animal story is an 'allegory', the situation in it is similar to our lives. In other words it allows a parallel between two situations to be drawn and the fun and learning is in considering all the implications of this.

We are going, at some point in the course of the drama, to adopt the role of an animal. As always, that does not mean we will act like a *particular* animal. Instead we will focus on the *attitude* of that role. So we still need to work at our level.

(Having said this to a senior adult group, an infant class would enjoy physically being the animals).

GAME

Everyone stand up. Each person think of an animal that possibly lives in a tropical rainforest. One other thing, the name of it has to have the same first letter as your first or second name. e.g. mine could be 'Allan anteater' or 'Owens orangutang'. When you have thought of a name, sit down. It will be harder for some of you than others. If you are really stuck, the group will help you but you have final choice of animal.

Go round the circle and listen to everyone's name. Get the rest of the class

110

to help those who are stuck. Reassure those who have picked the same animal that it is okay to have four leopards or two snakes, it is fine for the drama.

<table>
<tr><td>

DEFINING SPACE

</td><td>

You need a piece of material with just a little more than enough space for two people to lie down on (if this can be African material, or even one of the beautiful prints from Ghana, so much the better). As you are unfolding this and laying it down, ask the class to:

> Keep those animal roles ready but for a while I'd like you just to put them to the back of your mind whilst I tell you the dilemma story we are going to explore. It is called 'The Rains'. In some parts of Africa it is traditional for stories to be passed from one person to another, and from one generation to the next, not by books but by telling them. Try to remember all the details in this story. As well as using it in drama, you might want to pass it on to someone else in the future.

</td></tr>
<tr><td>

STORY-TELLING

</td><td>

Tell this story emphasising the sections in bold. These are the 'minute particularities' which will provide the constraints and tension for the drama to work. They focus the drama and have been put in place for that purpose. If you can tell the story rather than read it, you will be emphasising the oral tradition the story comes from.

</td></tr>
<tr><td>

KEY QUESTION

</td><td>

> That is where the story ends... I'm going to take on the role of the porcupine sitting in the doorway. What can Squirrel do? Does anyone know what they think Squirrel can do?

As soon as someone begins to speak or raise a hand, ask them to come and sit next to you and tell the idea so everyone can hear.

</td></tr>
<tr><td>

CLARIFICATION OF FRAME

</td><td>

Recap the plan that has been told to you to make sure role, focus, situation and perspective are clear. Ask the person:

> Would you be prepared to try the idea and see if it works? In other words, adopt the role of the squirrel

</td></tr>
</table>

just for a short while?

If the person does not want to, ask if anyone else would come out and try that particular idea.

Just before you start:

> I warn you I'm not going to make this easy for you. You may not succeed but you will have tried. We might have to try out a lot of ideas before we get one that really works. I'm going to ask the rest of the class how successful they think it has been when you have finished or if things get stuck. Let's go back to the point where Porcupine says 'I don't have a problem. You do!' Okay? Any questions before we start?

TEACHER IN ROLE PLAY CLASS AS AUDIENCE READY TO COMMENTATE

Run the action from 'I don't have a problem. You do!' Play the role in whatever way you need to avoid being out-manoeuvred by Squirrel; e.g. if being aggressive is not allowing Squirrel to execute his plan, back off a little and change to low status saying things like 'But you invited me in here in the first place' or 'Come on, let's be friends, let's give it a go'. Any tactic to vary the pace and fun in this 'game' which should now be developing in the drama.

If violence is suggested e.g. 'Hit him with a stick' then try it and use questioning and narration to control the outcome e.g. make sure the person locates where the stick might be in Squirrel's home. Ask what it would be doing there. Once this is established, wait for the volunteer to reach for it then you take the initiative with the narrative.

> e.g. Squirrel reached carefully for the big cleaning brush, and when Porcupine turned over, raised it right above his head. As he brought it down with tremendous force Porcupine stuck out a huge thick quill and speared the brush. 'What are you doing, Squirrel?'

The tension and fun of seeing the squirrel trying to find an excuse or explain what he was doing, defuses the violent solution in laughter.

112

Similarly if the first proposed idea is 'Get a gun and shoot him' this has to be given some credibility. There are various options depending on how well you know the class and how much drama they have done. With a class that has done a lot, you may be able to simply ask the class as a whole if they want to pursue that one. They will probably say 'No, that's daft'. If the class has not done a lot, then their agenda might be that they want to see you deal with this idea. Refusing to look at it might suggest that you are only looking for 'your idea'. If you do take it on, treat it as a serious suggestion and begin questioning. 'Where might Squirrel go to get a gun because we know there is not one in his home as we would have heard about it in the story?' The drama then follows this idea and narration is used in just the same way as with the stick, to create laughter and reinforce the fact that force is going to be difficult with this big creature.

COMMENTARY ON ACTION	Well that was a good try. Well done. Did any of you who were watching think it succeeded in any way?

Keep the emphasis on commentary on that piece of action. As soon as another idea is raised, ask that person to come and sit next to you.

Repeat the procedure used with the first idea.

ROLE PLAY TEACHER IN ROLE FORUM	Let's rewind time. None of the last idea has taken place. Let's us go back to the line 'I don't have a problem. You do!' Only this time, if you think a point is reached where Squirrel is again getting nowhere, shout out and stop the action. You have then quickly got to come in and try your idea. 'I don't have a problem. You do!'

Keep on trying solutions to this dilemma.

When a solution is finally found, follow up the consequences. For example, if the squirrel does manage by force, reason or trickery to get him out of his home, begin to narrate.

NARRATION	Porcupine went sliding down the muddy bank and disappeared into the swirling waters.

| TWO OPTIONS |

If you think he died as a result of having to leave or being thrown out, come and sit on this side of the room. If you think he was saved though perhaps injured, come and sit on this side of the room.

(The majority decision will be used later)

| NARRATION |

Let us rewind the drama to the moment when porcupine is forced, shoved, or just slips as he is leaving the home. Will someone be the squirrel? Which animal was the ruler of this forest?

Take whatever animal they say..

so Porcupine was swept down into the swirling waters...just as the King of the forest walked round the corner.

Mime walking around and looking shocked.

I saw you do that, you forced/let that porcupine fall into the river. Is this the way we treat our fellow creatures in this kingdom? No, it is not!

See if the squirrel tries to defend himself. When appropriate cut the dialogue off with narration.

The ruler decided that the squirrel would appear before the parliament of all the animals in the forest.

| WHOLE GROUP ROLE PLAY |

Remind the class of the animals they matched to their names at the start of the session and ask them to play that role.

Most honoured parliament of animals. I bring before you the squirrel whose dishonourable deed I witnessed only one hour ago.

Recount the incident when you saw porcupine seemingly being forced / let

out into the rain and swirling river.

Porcupine has not yet been found. Some of you, I know by the look on your faces, believe him to be dead. Some of you hope he will have survived. At this very minute I have a search party out looking for him or his body. It is with a sad heart that I place this creature before you to question and decide upon the punishment that justice demands.

Role play runs. Play teacher in role as devil's advocate to make suggestions, try to stir up feelings and debate. If an injection of tension is needed, the porcupine could be found by using narration:

the search party returns and Porcupine is with them

or (depending on the group's decision)

the search party returns and Porcupine is not with them

Beckon to a group of pupils to quickly play these roles and whisper if Porcupine is dead or alive (using the majority class decision from earlier when they had two options). The whole role play is focusing on justice, hospitality, custom, etc. Elevate your role's use of language whenever possible to give weight to these concepts.

REVIEW THE ROLE PLAY DISCUSSION

What was our drama really looking at besides the simple story of animals in a rain forest?

Get the group to try to articulate concepts and understandings outside the drama. Diagnostically, it is interesting to see who can drop their role at this point. Often individuals have become 'locked in their role' and it is a challenge to get them to discuss the concepts objectively, not in the drama. This is in itself a useful teaching point.

SMALL GROUP PLAY ALLEGORY ANALOGY

In groups of 3-5, devise a short piece of theatre that directly parallels the situation in the African story we have just been looking at. Some have already been mentioned (they will have come up in discussion naturally perhaps stimulated by an example from you).

Point out that the key content moments are:

1   The arrival of 'an unwanted guest' in whatever context you choose.

2   The moment when the equivalent of the line 'I don't have a problem. You do!' is spoken.

3   The resolution of the situation.

4   As far as form is concerned, how are you going to condense the great length of time involved to make the piece feel credible? You will have to consider what techniques/conventions/strategies you could use to do this.

5   The whole theatrical piece should be ten minutes long at the maximum.

DEVISING AND REHEARSAL TIME

Support and challenge the groups on the quality of the parallel they are drawing and the effectiveness of form used to convey ideas. This could be given a substantial amount of time given the quality of the initial pretext. Perhaps two weeks work before the pieces are performed in front of the rest of the group. Introduce lighting, music, set design etc.

PERFORMANCE OF THEATRE PIECES

The class are reminded of the original key content and structural moments. The pieces are watched with the rest of the class as audience.

DISCUSSION AND FEEDBACK

Content and form are reflected upon as a whole group.

Branch Planning for Different Ages

Senior school pupils & adults:

DEVISING, SCRIPT READING AND REHEARSAL

Discuss and share examples of other allegories used in plays. e.g. *The Insect Play* Brothers Copeck; *Animal Farm* adapted from George Orwell; *Metamorphosis* Steven Berkoff; etc. Either explore and perform extracts from these or devise another short piece of theatre using allegory.

KINAESTHETIC SCULPTURE

Move into poetic action. Build a monument or kinaesthetic sculpture for 'All those who are treated badly because they are kind' or 'Against all those who outstay their welcome' or 'Justice' or whatever concept figures most strongly in the particular drama.

Early years:

SONG & SOUND

Use song and sound to finish the session.

(To the tune of 'Frère Jacques')

> I hear thunder
> I hear thunder
> Hark don't you?
> Hark don't you?
> Pitter patter raindrops
> Pitter patter raindrops
> I'm wet through
> So are you

In a circle play 'The sound of rain game':-

> Everyone in a circle. We are going to try to use our
> imagination to make the sound of a rain storm passing

across a dense rainforest. It starts very slowly, slowly builds in noise and then slowly fades away until the last drops fall from the leaves. I will start with the first sounds and then one at a time, from my left, join in. We will really be passing the noise and the action. Any questions?

Action 1 – wash hands together.
Action 2 – fingers tap each other.
Action 3 – fingers tap the floor.
Action 4 – hands slap continuously on knees.
Action 5 – hands slap continuously and loudly on the floor.
Action 6 – feet stamp continuously on the floor.

Then reverse actions 6, 5, 4, 3, 2, 1... until the last person (next to you) quietly stops washing her hands. Repeat once more. Before repeating, ask the group, now that they have played the game, to really try to imagine the rain slowly starting, building up until it is so loud that it sounds like feet stamping and then slowly passing on, leaving the forest drenched and silent for a moment before the animal noises begin (possible next activity – soundtrack of the rainforest).

The Rains

Step	Reason	Convention	Emphasis
1 Let the class know this is a dilemma story that they will be able to finish	Clarifies nature of task	Contract and lesson outline	Establish the credibility of story /animals as a means to learn/ by all ages in parts of Africa
2 Tell the story	Creates atmosphere and sets pretext	Story-telling	No possibility of extending home/No chance of survival without one/Porcupine's superior strength
3 Use material to define the burrow area	Defines space - prevents superficial solutions	Defining space	Can't go above, behind, side, below
4 Will someone take on role of Squirrel? Teacher in role as Porcupine	Gets initial involvement. Most safely watch	Teacher-in-role/simple forum	Remind group of Squirrel's physical weakness and rain
5 'What are you going to do?'	Clarifies task. Stops embarrassment. Involves others	Discussion	Check it ties in with all facts known so far
6 Run action from 'I don't have a problem. You do'	Gives chance to be spectators	Role play. Narration	Use narration as a control device to avoid superficial response
7 'Does anyone else have a solution?'	Draws others into the drama	Discussion	Keep praising suggestions but emphasise difficulties
8 Review possible solutions if one does not work	Increases involvement	Role play in forum	Keep using narration to control and praise attempts
9 Run situations until one does work	Gives a sense of a valid effort	Discussion	Refer to the 'game of drama' (G. Bolton) out-witting – 'out thinking'
10 Could you construct a real life analogy or parallel? Can you think of one?	Brings the learning into focus	Discussion. Small or whole group play making	Insist on parallel e.g. customs, capture the moment when you say 'It's been good but you've got to go!'

Branch Planning:

Possibilities of whole class solution to *'Rains'* dilemma.

Whole group parallel in forum.

Possibility of moving into poetic action e.g. a monument, a poem, a kinaesthetic sculpture for 'All those who outstay their welcome' or 'All those who are treated badly because of kindness'.

Footnotes

1   Cecily O'Neill speaking at the National Drama Conference held at the London Institute of Education in 1993. The definition of the word pretext used in this book is based on our interpretation and understanding of the term from that speech. For other reading on the way Cecily O'Neill has subsequently developed her concept of 'pre-text' see: O'Neill,C. 1995 *Other Worlds*, Heinemann USA

Taylor, P. 1995 *Pre-text and Story drama – The Artistry of Cecily O'Neill and David Booth*, Monograph 1 n Publ. NADIE Administrator, Metro Arts Building, 109, Edward Street, Brisbane, Australia

For example: "A pre-text has a much more precise structural function than merely to propose an idea for dramatic exploration. The purpose of the pre-text is to activate the weaving of the text of the drama, because although the drama may not originate in a text, it always generates a text in action. Like a play in the theatre, the text generated by the process is an outcome, a dramatic product, and may be recalled and to some extent repeated." (p.41)

2   Cecily O'Neill spells pre-text with a hyphen. We have been more literal in our interpretation and definition and spell it without. To us a pretext approximates closely to the dictionary definition of the word. It is 'an ostensible reason, an excuse, the means' through which a group embarks on a drama. It may become central to the whole project or may fade to a common reference point from which the drama was launched.

3   For example:

- 'The Way West' in Lambert, A. and O'Neill, C. 1979 *Drama Structures*, Heinemann.

- 'A Village Under Threat' in Davies, G. 1983 *Practical Primary Drama* Heinemann.

- 'The Pied Piper' in Woolland, B. 1992 *Drama in the Primary School* Longman

Mike Fleming gives a full appendix section to a list of such structures (Fleming, M. 1994 *Starting Drama Teaching*, David Fulton Publ. Appendix B p.177-178). He comments: 'It is nearly always enriching to read about the practical work of other teachers but rarely possible to use ideas without some modification to suit different contexts and specific objectives.'

We agree with the points about modification but believe that pretexts such as these are more than just examples of practical work. They can be used as texts by others and should not be confined to the appendix. They are central to any discussion about the drama education process.

4   HMI 1990 *The Teaching and Learning of Drama*, HMSO. Journals such as *Research in Drama Education* are contributing much to the quality of debate about the nature and function of learning through, in and about drama. (Somers, J. Edit. *Research in Drama Education*, Vol.1. 1995 Carfax Publ.)

5   'sit - stillery' was a phrase used by Henry Caldwell Cook in 1917 (Caldwell Cook, H. 1917 *The PlayWay – an Essay in Educational Method*, Heinemann)

6   Hughes K. Nov 1994 *Teaching Learners, Learning Teachers, Teaching and Democracy* in *Adults Learning* Publ. NIACE Vol.6 No 3

7   Neelands, J. 1993 *Teaching Without Walls*, Drama, National Drama Publishing

8   See for example Bruner, J. 1986 *Actual Minds, Possible Worlds*, H.U.P.or Donaldson, M. 1978 *Children's Minds*, Fontana

9   Caldwell Cook, H. 1917 *The PlayWay*, Heinemann

    Finlay Johnson, H. 1923 *The Dramatic Method of Teaching*, Heinemann

    Slade, P. 1954 *Child Drama*, Univ. London Press

    Way, B. 1967 *Development Through Drama*, Longman

    Johnson, L. O'Neill, C. 1984 *Dorothy Heathcote: Collected Writings*, Hutchinson

    Bolton, G. 1991 *New Perspectives on Classroom Drama*, Simon & Schuster

    Neelands, J. 1983 *Making Sense of Drama*, Heinemann

    Barton, B. & Booth, D. 1990 *Stories in the Classroom*, Pembroke Publ.

    O'Toole, J. 1992 *The Process of Drama*, Routledge

10 Mike Fleming makes this point very clearly: 'A mistake made by drama practitioners in the past was to assume that there is a necessary causal connection between particular methodologies in drama and work of quality'. (Flemming, M. 1994 *Starting Drama Teaching*, David Fulton Publ.) Interestingly he also points out that an approach through semiotics ...' the way sign systems of drama, words, expression, gesture, lighting, music and so on, combine to communicate meaning to an audience...can neglect to recognise the importance of our sensory engagement with the theatre. Attention to structures and signs, focuses attention on what might be termed "objective dimensions" but does not describe the experience of the participants in the exercise.' pp.166-167.

11 Nicoll, A. 1927 *The Development of the Theatre*, George C. Harrap & Co. Ltd.

12 Taylor, P. (Edit.) 1995 *Pre-text and Story Drama*, NADIE Publ. p.20

13 For detailed information about conventions see: Neelands, J. 1990 *Structuring Drama Work* C.U.P. Conventions are classified in this work and an established and accepted title is given for each. Whilst acknowledging these, we also include various other titles by which they are known.

14 For a detailed explanation of metaxis see: Boal, A. 1979 *The Theatre of the Oppressed*, Pluto Press

Drama Education Associations, Organisations & Publications

Publications only are marked with a *

All other entries are associations and organisations which also produce publications, often from conferences and courses they run.

Centre for Studies in Drama in Education, Faculty of Education, University of Central England in Birmingham, Westbourne Road, Edgbaston, Birmingham, B15 3TN

Dorothy Heathcote Archive* – University of Lancaster, Lancaster LA1 4YL.

Dorothy Heathcote Catalogue* – Audio Visual Centre, University of Newcastle, The Medical School, Framlington Place, Newcastle upon Tyne, NE2 4HH

International Drama Education Researchers Network, School of Education, University of Exeter, Exeter, Devon EX1 2LU

Local Drama Associations – there are many local associations throughout the UK which provide valuable support networks. For example:

> **Cheshire Association for Drama Education,** (CADE), Cheshire Drama Resource Centre, Verdin Centre, High Street, Winsford, Cheshire CW7 2AY

> **East of Scotland Drama Association,** Linda Boyle, 31 Easter Livilands, Stirling, FK7 0BQ

> **Norfolk Network for the Teaching of Drama,** Centre for Arts in Education, Bull Close Road, Norwich NR3 1NG

> **London Drama,** Holborn Centre for Performing Arts, 3 Cups Yard, Sandland Street, London WC1R 4PZ

National Association for Drama in Education - Australia, PO Box 163, Albert Street, Brisbane, Queensland 4002 Australia

National Association of Teachers of Drama, Sorrel Oates, Membership Secretary, 13 Austin Street, Northhampton. NN1 3EY

National Drama, Paul Kaverman, Membership Secretary, 4 Hollin Drive, Leeds, West Yorkshire LS16 5NE

New Theatre Quarterly,* The Edinburgh Building, Shaftesbury Road, Cambridge, CB2 2RU

The Standing Conference on Young People's Theatre, Ian Yeoman & Chris Cooper, The Dukes Theatre, Moor Lane, Lancaster, LA1 1QE

National Foundation for Arts Education, Michael Cahill, Westminster College, Oxford OX2 9AT

Research in Drama Education,* Carfax Publishing Company, PO Box 25, Abingdon, Oxfordshire, OX14 3UE

Scottish Drama, Moray House Publications, Moray House Institute of Education, Holyrood Road, Edinburgh, EH8 8AQ

Shakespeare in Schools,* Rex Gibson, University of Cambridge Institute of Education, Shaftesbury Road, Cambridge, CB2 2BX

2D Dance & Drama*, 33 Cannock Street, Leicester, LE4 7HR

Theatre in Prisons and Probation Centres, James Thompson, Manchester University Drama Dept, Oxford Road, Manchester, M14 6HD

Ulster Drama, Alma Lutton, 3 Lincoln Heights, Sheep Hill, Ballymeena, BT42 1QR

Illustrative Booklist

if you are interested in reading more about Drama Education

Abbs. P.1989 *The Symbolic Order,* The Falmer Press

Allen, J. 1979 *Drama in Schools,* Heinemann

Aston, E. & Savona, G. 1991 *Theatre as a Sign System,* Routledge

Barker, C. 1980 *Theatre Games,* Methuen

Best, D 1992 *The Rationality of Feeling: Understanding the Arts in Education,* The Falmer Press

Boal, A. 1979 *Theatre of the Oppressed,* Pluto

Boal, A. 1992 *Games for Actors and Non-Actors,* Routledge

Boal, A. 1995 *The Rainbow of Desire,* Routledge

Barlow, S. & Skidmore S. 1995 *Drama Form,* Hodder & Stoughton

Barrett, S. 1995 *It's All Talk,* Carel Press

Bolton, G. 1979 *Towards a Theory of Drama Education,* Longman

Bolton, G. 1984 *Drama as Education,* Longman

Bolton, G. 1991 *New Perspectives on Classroom Drama,* Simon & Schuster

Barton, B. & Booth, D. 1990 *Stories in the Classroom,* Pembroke Publ.

Burgess, R. & Gaudrey, P. 1985 *Time for Drama,* Longman

Byron, K. 1986 *Drama in the English Classroom,* Methuen

Caldwell Cook, H. 1917 *The PlayWay,* Heinemann

Calouste Gulbenkian Foundation 1982 *The Arts in Schools,* Calouste Gulbenkian Foundation Publ.

Courtenay, R. 1965 *Teaching Drama,* Cassell

Courtenay, R. 1974 *Play Drama and Thought,* Cassell

Courtenay, R. 1980 *The Dramatic Curriculum,* Heinemann

Cox, M. (Ed) 1992 *Shakespeare Comes to Broadmoor,* Jessica Kingsley Publ.

Davies, D. & Lawrence, C. 1986 *Gavin Bolton: Selected Writings,* Longman

Davies, G. 1983 *Practical Primary Drama,* Heinemann

Day, C. & Norman, J. 1983 *Issues in Educational Drama,* Falmer Press

Evans, T. 1985 *Drama in English Teaching,* Croom Helm

Fairclough, J. 1996 *A Teacher's Guide to History through Role Play,* English Heritage Publ.

Fines, J. & Verrier, R. 1974 *The Drama of History,* New Univ. Education

Finlay Johnson, H. 1923 *The Dramatic Method of Teaching,* Nesbit

Griffiths, D. 1991 *An Early Start to Drama,* Simon & Schuster

Hargreaves, D.(Edit) 1989 *Children and the Arts,* O.U.P.

Heathcote, D. & Bolton, G. 1995 *Drama for Learning: An Account of Dorothy Heathcote's Mantle of the Expert,* USA Heinemann

Hodgson, J. & Banham, M. (Eds) 1971-75 *Drama in Education – The Annual Survey,* Vols 1/2/3 Pitman

Hodgson, J. 1972 *The Uses of Drama,* Methuen

Hornbrook, D. 1989 *Education and Dramatic Art,* Blackwell Educ.

Hornbrook, D. 1991 *Education in Drama,* Falmer Press

Jackson, T. 1993 *Learning Through Theatre,* Routledge

Jennings, S. 1973 *Remedial Drama,* Pitman

Jennings, S. 1986 *Creative Drama in Group Work,* Winslow Press

Jennings, S. 1987 *Dramatherapy Theory and Practice,* Jessica Kingsley Press

Jennings, S. 1992 *Dramatherapy Theory and Practice 2,* Jessica Kingsley Press

Jennings, S. 1993 *Introduction to Dramatherapy,* Jessica Kingsley Press

Jennings, S. 1994 *The Handbook of Dramatherapy,* Routledge

Johnson, L. & O'Neill, C. 1984 *Dorothy Heathcote: Collected Writings,* Hutchinson

Kempe, A. 1988 *The Drama Sampler,* Blackwell

Kempe, A. 1990 *The GCSE Drama Course Book,* Blackwell

Kershaw, B. 1992 *The Politics of Performance,* Routledge

Langer, S. 1953 *Feeling and Form,* Routledge & Keegan Paul

Linnel, R. 1982 *Approaching Classroom Drama,* Edward Arnold

Linnel, R. 1988 *Practical Drama Handbook,* Hodder & Stoughton

Linnel, R. 1991 *Theatre Arts Workbook,* Hodder & Stoughton

Marston, P., Brockbank, K., McGuire, B., Morton, S. 1990 *Drama 14-16,* Stanley Thornes

McGregor, L. Tate, M. & Robinson K. 1977 *Learning Through Drama,* Heinemann

Motter, T.H.V. 1929 *The School Drama in England,* Longman

Morton, D. 1984 *Drama for Capability,* Kemble Press

Morgan, N. & Saxton, J. (1987) *Teaching Drama,* Hutchinson

Neelands, J. 1983 *Making Sense of Drama,* Heinemann

Neelands, J. 1990 *Structuring Drama Work,* C.U.P.

Neelands, J. 1992 *Learning Through Imagined Experience,* Hodder & Stoughton

Neelands, J. 1993 *Drama and I.T. The Human Dimension,* NATE & NCET

Nixon, J. 1987 *Teaching Drama,* Macmillan Educ.

O'Neill, C. 1995 *Other Worlds,* Heinemann USA

O'Neill, C. & Lambert, A. 1984 *Drama Structures,* Hutchinson

O'Neill, C., Lambert, A., Linnel, R. & Warr-Wood, J. 1976 *Drama Guidelines,* Heinemann

O'Toole, J. 1977 *Theatre in Education,* Hodder & Stoughton

O'Toole, J. & Haseman, B. 1987 *Drama Wise – An Introduction to GCSE,* Heinemann

O'Toole, J. 1992 *The Process of Drama,* Routledge

Pemberton-Billing, R. & Clegg, J. 1965 *Teaching Drama,* Univ. London Press

Peter, M. 1994 *Drama for all,* David Fulton Publ

Peter, M. 1994 *Making Drama Special,* David Fulton Publ

Readman, G. Lamont G. Drama: *A Handbook for Primary Teachers,* 1994 BBC Books

Roberts, T. 1988 *Special Needs in Ordinary Schools – Arts in the Primary Curriculum,* Cassel

Ross, M. 1978 *The Creative Arts,* Heinemann

Ross, M. 1984 *The Development of Aesthetic Experience,* Pergammon

Robinson, K. 1980 *Exploring Theatre & Education,* Heinemann

Schechner, R. 1988 *Performance Theory,* Routledge

Slade, P. 1954 *Child Drama,* Univ London Press

Slade, P. 1958 *An Introduction to Child Drama,* Univ. London Press

Slade, P. 1968 *Experience in Spontaneity,* Longman

Somers, J. 1994 *Drama in the Curriculum,* Cassell

Stabler, T. 1979 *Drama in the Primary Schools,* Heinemann

Swartz, L. 1988 *A Practical Guide for Teaching Drama,* Pembroke

Taylor, K. (Edit) 1991 *Drama Strategies,* Heinemann

Taylor P. (Edit) 1996 *Researching Drama and Art Education,* Falmer Press

Tomlinson, R. 1982 *Disability, Theatre and Education,* Condor

Turner, V. 1992 *From Ritual to Theatre – The Human Seriousness of Play,* P.J.A. Publ

Wagner, B.J. 1979 Dorothy Heathcote – *Drama as a Learning Medium,* Hutchinson

Watkins, B. 1981 *Drama and Education,* Batsford

Way, B. 1967 *Development Through Drama,* Longman

White, D. & Williams, J. (eds). 1992 *Ways with Plays,* Carel Press

Witkin, R. 1974 *The Intelligence of Feeling,* Heinemann

Woolland, B. 1993 *The Teaching of Drama in the Primary School,* Longman

Wooton, M. (Edit) 1982 *New directions in Drama Teaching,* Heinemann